LONDON

Contents

Contents by Region

Introduction

T ime spent in London is something few visitors ever forget. The enormity of the city overwhelms and carries one along in a truly memorable fashion. It is not simply the size of the city that contributes to this enormity, but the diversity of the culture, the wealth of opportunities and the overall richness of the experience. Merely by standing on a cobbled street, you know you are at the hub of one of the oldest, most historically fascinating, cities in the world. There has been a settlement here since time immemorial. We know, from written history, of the tribes that were living here when the Romans arrived, but there are also archaeological signs telling us of much earlier civilisations that relied heavily upon the River Thames for their livelihood. Ancient people were drawn here just as we are today – there is something almost magnetic in London's attraction.

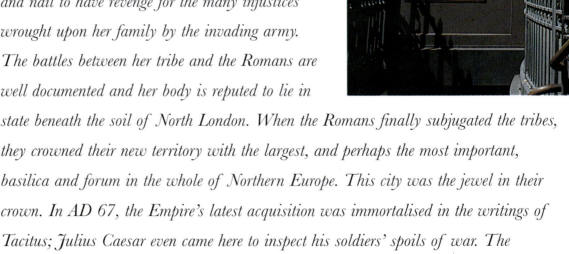

For many years, the Romans and the indigenous tribes fought over the land that is now London. Perhaps the most furious of all the Romans' opponents was the much-wronged Boudicca, who fought tooth and nail to have revenge for the many injustices wrought upon her family by the invading army. The battles between her tribe and the Romans are well documented and her body is reputed to lie in

state beneath the soil of North London. When the Romans finally subjugated the tribes, they crowned their new territory with the largest, and perhaps the most important, basilica and forum in the whole of Northern Europe. This city was the jewel in their crown. In AD 67, the Empire's latest acquisition was immortalised in the writings of Tacitus; Julius Caesar even came here to inspect his soldiers' spoils of war. The Romans named this area 'Londinium'; there is also evidence to suggest that a similar name, 'Lyn-dun', was already in use at this time.

The Romans began what centuries of residents and invaders were to continue – the building of one of the world's most significant cities. Before the arrival of William the Conqueror, many English kings added to the importance of this vital fortification. Alfred the Great, for one, began an extensive rebuilding programme, ensuring the nation was adequately defended from this strategic vantage point. At that time, the River Thames was a great deal larger and wider than it is today and invaders from the sea were common. Alfred also helped develop the area now known as the City of London. It covers one square mile and then, as now, was an important centre of business.

Since the time of William I, London and its surrounding area has been the seat of the monarch and this south-easterly location rapidly became accepted as the country's capital city. Many of England's most important events have taken place here: from the beheading of Charles I to the first nights of Shakespeare's plays; from the founding of the Royal Academy to the imprisonment of Elizabeth I in the Tower of London. Rossetti painted here, Keats wrote here, Handel composed here and the Beatles recorded here. Generations of eminent, as well as notorious, citizens have made London their home, whether they hoped to gain recognition or anonymity – either is possible in this fascinating, and sometimes overwhelming, place.

For years, visitors to London have decided to remain and live amongst its boiling pot of personalities: conquerors and refugees, rich and poor, of every race and every tongue. From the Normans to the Huguenots, Jews to Lutherans, Bangladeshis to West Indians; people of all languages, creeds and colours have come here, hoping to find a new life. Even the Thames, the centre of the settlement, derives the pronunciation of its

name from a foreign tongue: William may have conquered the country but he was unable to conquer the language; he found 'th' far too difficult so, from being pronounced exactly as it is spelt, the name of London's river changed to the name still in use today. In true French fashion the 'h' was ignored and the 'Thames' became the 'Tems'.

The extraordinary magic of London lies in its striking diversity and its many different guises, centred on the ubiquitous mix of old and new apparent everywhere one looks. The anomaly of a city famed for its greenness; the bold fusion of twentieth-century architecture alongside eleventh-century churches; the opulence of Regency theatres alongside the simplicity of sixteenth-century pubs. It is the same as, and the opposite of, everything one looks for.

Whatever you enjoy doing you can do in London: from horse-riding to rollerblading, river cruises to nightclubbing; from open-air concerts to indoor go-carting; tea at the Ritz to beers in Soho; Harrods to Portobello Road. The choice is

endless. In London you can hear every language of the world spoken all around you, see every type of skin colour, eat any national cuisine under the sun, visit a different theatre – fringe or mainstream – every night for a year. Tour Buckingham Palace or visit an East End market; go to the opera or go to carnival; sunbathe in the royal parks or go Christmas shopping in the snow. Some activities are free and some can cost a fortune – the choice is yours.

When it rains no city looks its best, but even in inclement weather London has many compensations: finding a cosy pub to shelter from the rain, visiting one of the capital's fantastic museums, dining exquisitely in a warm restaurant, sipping coffee in a bookshop café. And when the sun shines, there are few cities on earth to rival London: the deep blue sky, the rich green of the numerous parks and gardens, the scent of a fresh-flower market stall.

The magic and mystery of London is evident all around when one looks up above the bright lights of the shops and cafés, and realises that the street so thronged with life today was once the home of a famous, impoverished

composer, or a brilliant inventor, perhaps the mistress of the King lived here or the ghost of a jilted lover. The streets are brimming with history unknown to the majority of residents and tourists. So many millions of people have lived here over the centuries that the paving stones and house bricks could relate more stories than you could possibly hear in your own lifetime. Stories of famous residents, such as Wat Tyler, Samuel Pepys, Christopher Wren, Wolfgang Amadeus Mozart, Walter Sickert and Charles Dickens, as well as the more unpleasant side to life in the city, such as the horror caused by Jack the Ripper or the plight of the many thousands who died during the Black Death. Beneath every paving stone on which you walk lie more decades of history than days in a year, behind every stone facade is the story of lives gone by, both sensational and

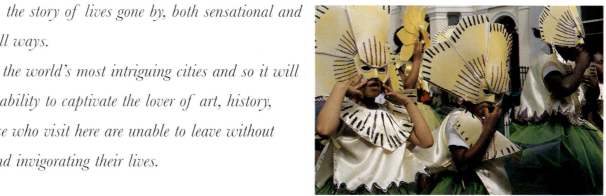

mediocre, but fascinating in all ways.

London remains one of the world's most intriguing cities and so it will remain because of its unique ability to captivate the lover of art, history, mystery and excitement. Those who visit here are unable to leave without enriching their imagination and invigorating their lives.

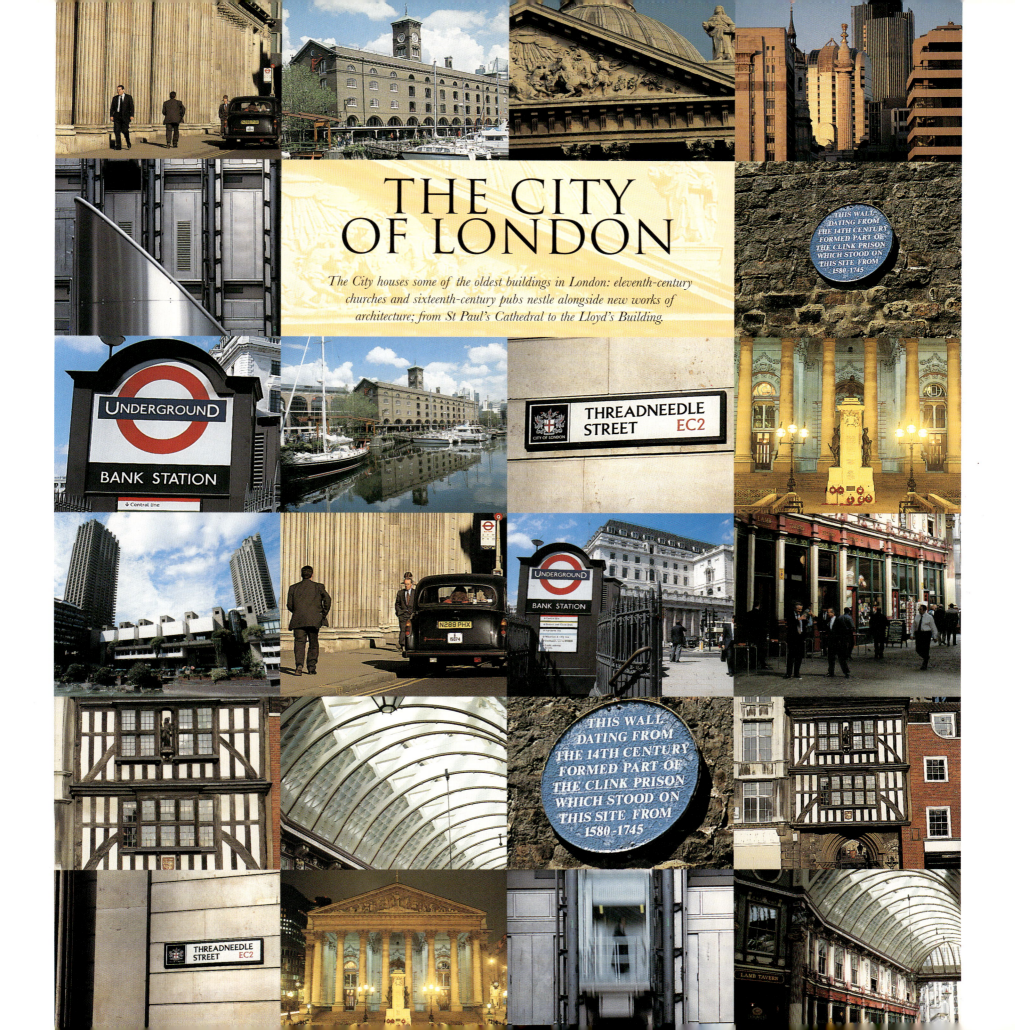

THE CITY OF LONDON

The City houses some of the oldest buildings in London: eleventh-century churches and sixteenth-century pubs nestle alongside new works of architecture; from St Paul's Cathedral to the Lloyd's Building.

Bank of England
BARTHOLOMEW LANE, EC2

to promote ... the publick Good and Benefit of our people.

Charter of the Bank of England, 1694

The Bank of England, affectionately nicknamed 'the Old Lady of Threadneedle Street', opened in 1694. The idea of a national bank was proposed by a Scotsman, William Paterson (1658-1710); who became the Bank's first Director. Paterson took the idea from Amsterdam, where the first Dutch bank had opened in 1609. Today the Bank of England remains the centre of England's financial world ensuring the integrity of the country's currency and financial institutions.

In 1788, the task of recreating the building which housed the Bank was allotted to the master architect Sir John Soane (1753-1837). He worked on the project for 45 years, completing the building in various stages. The first of his designs to see fruition was the Bank Stock Office, which was completed in 1793. Soane was also responsible for several other magnificent buildings around London, perhaps the most famous of these is the Dulwich Picture Gallery – a stunning piece of architecture and the first public art gallery to open in Britain.

Barbican Centre
EC2

The Barbican Centre for Arts and Conferences was a gift to the nation from the Corporation of London. The multi-million pound project was first discussed in the 1960s and finally opened by the Queen in 1982. It contains a concert hall, two theatres, three cinemas, two art galleries and a public library. There are also places to eat and relax and the centre often plays host to conferences and exhibitions. The enormous arts complex provides pleasant walks, bookshops, free entertainment and bars that are open to the public. On a lazy Sunday afternoon visitors can listen to free concerts while soaking up the ambience of a city at leisure.

The Barbican area was so heavily blitzed during the Second World War that little of its original architecture remains; however, it is one of the oldest parts of London and the remains of the original city wall can be seen just a few minutes' walk away. The present network of buildings, which includes flats and shops, covers an area of 20 acres. At the highest level (of ten) is the roof-top conservatory. It houses over 2,000 species of plants, not to mention an aviary and ponds full of exotic fish.

St Bartholomew's Gatehouse
LITTLE BRITAIN, EC1

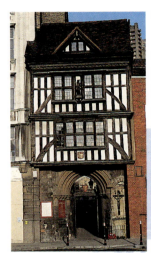

The old church of St Bartholomew the Great dates back to 1123, when it was founded by a royal courtier named Rahere; his tomb can be found before the High Altar. After a near-fatal illness, the dissolute Rahere underwent a conversion to Christianity and saw a vision of St Bartholomew. He built the church to thank God for sparing his life.

Many parts of the original building remain standing today and St Bartholomew the Great's is now the oldest church in the City of London – the only one of its age to survive the Great Fire of 1666. The church was also threatened during the Dissolution of the Monasteries; indeed, many parts of the building were pulled down under the orders of Henry VIII, but fortuitously the oldest parts escaped destruction.

The gatehouse seen in this picture was constructed in 1559. It is built in the Tudor style of the time and remains beautifully preserved – this is due in part to the later façade which hid the original gatehouse from view for many years. The Tudor building was only revealed during the First World War, when a Zeppelin bomb blew off the outer covering of bricks.

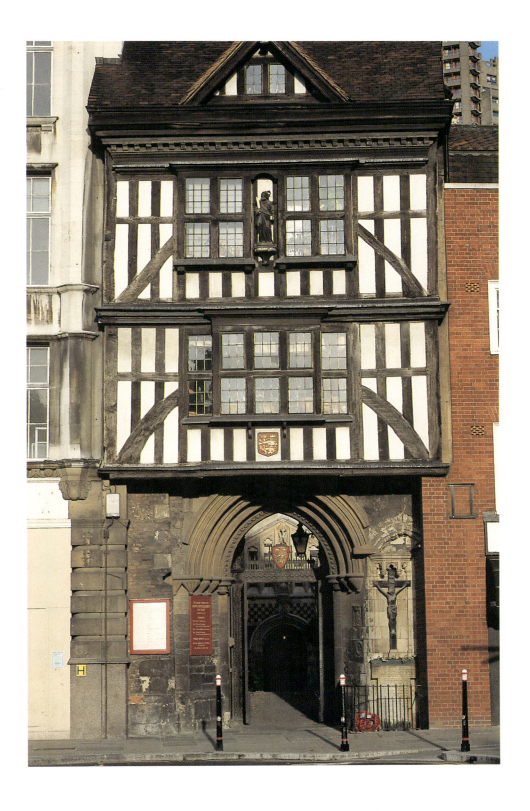

The Clink Prison
SOUTHWARK, SE1

The Clink Prison no longer exists, but on its former site stands a museum which exhibits information about the gaol. The Clink (from whose name the slang term 'clink' meaning 'prison' arose) dates back to the early sixteenth century. Its first inmates were prisoners of conscience. The conditions were appalling and vicious forms of torture commonplace. More muted forms of punishment included prisoners being put in the stocks, whipped or suffering the ducking stool.

The prison was ruled by the Bishop of Winchester, whose palace stood alongside the gaol, on what is now named Clink Street. The palace was demolished during the Civil War, but its magnificent fourteenth-century rose window still remains in one of the semi-tumbled walls.

During the seventeenth century, the prison became a more general gaol, housing murderers, debtors, drunkards and street fighters alongside the religious prisoners. The proliferation of theatres in Southwark at the time led to a great many drunken brawls, excessive gambling and general rowdiness. Many over-zealous theatregoers found themselves in the Clink after a particularly riotous evening. Records survive of numerous payments made to bail actors who were needed back on stage.

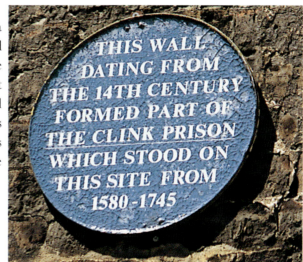

Lloyds Building
LIME STREET, EC3

The Lloyd's Building is one of London's most important examples of Post-Modern architecture. The vast construction (one of whose lift shafts can be seen here) houses one of the world's premier insurance companies, Lloyd's of London. The building, designed by the architect Richard Rogers, encompasses over 100,000 sq ft of office space and was opened in 1986.

Lloyd's of London was founded in the seventeenth century; the company moved to Lime Street in the 1920s. Lloyd's first home was a coffee house kept by Edward Lloyd which rapidly became the accepted place for businessmen and merchants to meet and trade. Gradually it also became the haunt of underwriters, whose business was to provide insurance for ships leaving London. In 1696, Edward began to distribute *Lloyd's News*, superseded in 1734 by *Lloyd's List*.

The area around Lime Street has been of great importance for many centuries. Not far away is Undershaft – the site of a maypole in medieval times and, for many decades, the centre of the local community.

Leadenhall Market
EC2

eadenhall Market, one of the City of London's few remaining markets, stands on the site of London's ancient Roman forum and basilica. A market has been held on this site since the fourteenth century, when it was a renowned place to buy and sell livestock; it was eventually expanded to sell other goods. The present building, designed by Horace Jones, dates back to 1881; the market's name, however, comes from an earlier house that stood on this site, whose roof was made of lead.

Not far away are the remains of an ancient temple dedicated to Mithras, a Persian god who became assimilated into Roman religion. In 1889, a depiction of the god was discovered; the inscription on the relief indicating that it had been dedicated by a soldier of the II Legio Augusta. This find led to the belief that a temple must be nearby. However, these suspicions were to remain unconfirmed in the lifetimes of those who strove to find it. It was not until 1954, during an excavation of a Second World War bomb-site, that the foundations of a temple were uncovered. Items since discovered here have been dated to the second century.

Monument
EC2

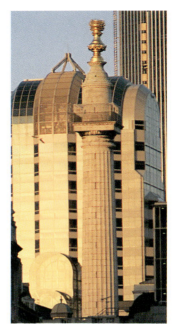

Jane called us up, about 3 in the morning, to tell us of a great fire they saw in the City.... By and by Jane comes and tells me that she hears that above 300 houses have been burned down tonight by the fire we saw, and that it was now burning down all Fishstreet.

Diary entry for 2 September 1666, Samuel Pepys

The Great Fire of London raged for 60 hours. When it finally burnt itself out it had destroyed 463 acres of land and had even spread outside the City walls. 13,200 houses were gone – incredibly, only nine people were known to have died.

The fire began in a baker's shop in Pudding Lane. The blaze apparently turned out to be an act of arson – a Frenchman named Robert Hubert confessed to starting it. He was hanged at the public execution spot of Tyburn.

While the city struggled to recover from the terrible destruction, it was decided that a monument be erected in memory of the fire and the appalling devastation it had caused. Sir Christopher Wren was chosen as its architect and it was unveiled, at the corner of what is now Fish Street Hill and Monument Street, in 1677.

The Royal Exchange
THREADNEEDLE STREET/CORNHILL, EC3

This area of London has been an area of prominence since Roman times and has had associations with trade for many centuries. The idea of an Exchange was inspired by the *Oude Beurs* in Antwerp, a place where traders from all countries could meet to do business.

The first Royal Exchange building was constructed on this site in 1566-67 by Thomas Gresham; it cost £3,532 17s. 2d. Gresham became a great favourite of Queen Elizabeth I, who gave the Exchange its first Royal seal of approval. During the Great Fire of London, the Exchange was burned down. Poignantly, the only item that remained unscathed was the statue of the architect.

A second Exchange was built in 1669, to a grand design by Edward Jarman; sadly Jarman died before he could see his work completed. In an eerie stroke of ill fate, Jarman's building also burned down, on 10 January 1838. The building seen today is the third Royal Exchange building, designed by William Tite and opened by Queen Victoria in 1844. Tite was later knighted for his efforts and Tite Street (SW3) was named after him – famous residents include Oscar Wilde, John Singer Sargent, Augustus John and James McNeill Whistler.

Bank Tube Station
EC2

Bank, situated in front of the Bank of England, is one of the City of London's most important tube stations. It is connected by tunnels to Monument station and between them they provide services on six different underground lines. Like all areas in the City, the streets around Bank are tremendously crowded during the week and almost deserted at the weekends.

The sign denoting a tube station is one of London's most well-known landmarks. There are 12 underground lines, including the Docklands Light Railway – this connects the heart of the City with the old docks, which are now a thriving business community. The original London Underground map dated from 1908, a time when the tube system was still very young and relatively small scale. In the early 1930s, Henry Beck designed the tube map that is still in use today. It revolutionised the way Londoners visualised the tube network, making it explicable and easy to use. Instead of concentrating the map on the true geography of London, he used approximations, straight lines and angles roughly to plot each area. His now-famous illustration has become the prototype for railway maps throughout the world and remains one of the classics of 1930s design.

St Katharine's Dock
E1

St Katharine's Dock takes its name from St Katharine's Hospital which once stood on this site. The hospital was founded in the twelfth century by the philanthropic Queen Matilda, the French wife of King Stephen (*c.* 1097-1154), who was the grandson of William the Conqueror.

The docks that later grew up here were designed by the Scottish engineer Thomas Telford and opened in 1828. They served as London's most central docks – within easy walking distance of the Tower of London – for 140 years. Throughout the nineteenth century, St Katharine's Dock was a bustle of activity, witnessing enormous amounts of precious cargo being loaded and unloaded on to the boards. However, like all London's docks, they were severely affected by the popularity of the railways and, later, air-freight systems. St Katharine's closed in 1968.

In 1973, Taylor Woodrow took over the area and transformed it into the successful residential and commercial centre it has become today. Facilities include a yacht marina, a hotel and the renowned World Trade Centre, and visitors to the docks can enjoy a variety of regular entertainment.

St Paul's Cathedral
EC4

A cathedral dedicated to St Paul dates back to the beginning of the seventh century, when Ethelbert, King of Kent, built one on this site. The building was destroyed in 1087 by fire. A replacement cathedral was begun at once, with encouragement from William the Conqueror – this second building was also the victim of fires: it was badly damaged in 1561 and utterly destroyed by the Great Fire of London in 1666.

The present-day St Paul's Cathedral was designed by Christopher Wren. His original plans also included grand surrounding streets and buildings, but sadly, lack of funds prevented his scheme from reaching fruition. During his work on the cathedral, Wren was knighted by King Charles II, however, despite royal recognition, Wren was treated very badly by the building committee. His superior designs took over 20 years to complete and he was accused of deliberately delaying completing his work in order to increase his payment. As a result, they docked his fee by fifty per cent.

St Paul's encompasses five chapels alongside the main body of the church; many fine statues and memorials; rich paintings, including *The Light of the World*; a crypt and the world-famous Whispering Gallery.

Threadneedle Street
EC2

Threadneedle Street, at the heart of the City of London, has been one of England's most important trading and financial centres since the time of the Romans, and possibly before. During the 1930s, excavations of the area unearthed Roman mosaics and pottery buried beneath the street's foundations.

The street's unusual name is usually attributed to the Guild of Merchant Taylors, whose building still stands in Threadneedle Street today. Other buildings on this illustrious road include the Bank of England, the Royal Exchange and the Stock Exchange.

The crest at the left-hand side of the road-name sign is the coat of arms of the Corporation of London. Every street sign within the City of London – a district that spans one square mile – bears that crest. The motto is *Domine dirige nos* ('Lord Guide Us'). The boundaries of the City are: Temple Bar and Holborn in the west; Smithfield and Moorfields in the north; the Thames in the south and Aldgate and Tower Hill in the east.

LONDON LIFE

From tea at the Ritz to bagels at Brick Lane Market, life in London is wonderfully diverse. Whether shopping on Oxford Street or taking a quiet walk through Hampstead, there is always something new and exciting to do.

Brick Lane
E1

Brick Lane, in London's East End, derives its name from the sixteenth century when this road was the centre of the brick- and tile-making industry. In the seventeenth century, the Black Eagle Brewery was built here and in the eighteenth century, Brick Lane became a farmers' market, selling livestock and fresh produce.

Its proximity to the river and the docks ensured that this area of London became home to large numbers of immigrants from all over the globe: French refugees, persecuted Jews and large numbers of immigrants from Asia. Today Brick Lane remains at the heart of the Bengali community. The first Bengalis to set up home here arrived as sailors working on the merchant ships importing goods from Asia.

The farmers' market tradition still carries on in Brick Lane and every Sunday morning visitors can find one of the city's most vibrant markets here. Customers can choose from a diverse selection of goods on sale: from fruit to furniture; from shoes to spices; from bric-a-brac to Bengali sweets; and from bicycles to freshly-baked bagels.

Camden Lock Market
CAMDEN, NW1

Camden Lock Market is one of five markets that are known collectively as Camden Market. The other four sections are: the Electric Market, the Canal Market, the Stables Market and Inverness Street Market. All five specialise in different wares and the choice is endlessly diverse. Inverness Street Market is open every day except Sunday; and the other four are open at weekends.

There are over 60 markets in London, but the one most natives choose to visit is Camden. It is a regular weekend meeting place for young Londoners and, as there is great nightlife to be found in the surrounding area, Camden remains vibrant even after the markets have closed.

Camden Lock, once a run-down area of disused warehouses, opened as a market in 1974. The inventively renovated buildings mean that the market is never rained off. Meanwhile, on sunny days, customers can enjoy eating and drinking alongside the Regent's Canal, while being entertained by buskers.

Second-Hand Bookshops
CECIL COURT, WC2

The pedestrianised Cecil Court and its adjoining Charing Cross Road are renowned for their second-hand and antiquarian bookshops. The shops themselves are reminiscent of an earlier age, many of them were book shops in the nineteenth century and the buildings' history goes back even further. Mozart is reputed to have stayed in Cecil Court in 1764. At the time, it was not a particularly salubrious residence – the area around Charing Cross Road was once one of London's most notorious slums.

The slums were cleared away in the late-nineteenth century when the road was redeveloped. It was required to be a wider, clearer thoroughfare than any previously constructed. At this time there were more carriages than ever before, and the advent of motor cars on the streets of London was just around the corner.

Not far away is Charing Cross station, which received its name because of its thirteenth-century Eleanor Cross (of which a replica stands in front of the station today). Eleanor was the wife of Edward I. After her death in 1290, her body was carried from Nottinghamshire to Westminster Abbey for burial. Afterwards, 12 crosses were erected to mark the places where the funeral party had stopped to rest during its journey.

The Holly Bush
HAMPSTEAD, NW3

Dictionaries are like watches.
The worst is better than none at all and even the best
cannot be expected to run quite true.
Dr Samuel Johnson

An inn has stood on this site since the early seventeenth century. Its name derives from an ancient tradition, in common practice during the pub's early days, of fixing a green branch above the door to advise potential customers that wine and beer was being sold here.

This is one of London's most authentic old pubs; in over 300 years, the interior has barely been changed and it was run by the same family for almost two centuries. Its famous clientele include the writers Dr Samuel Johnson and James Boswell and the painter George Romney, who lived at nearby Romney House. The artist, in what was at the time seen as a highly eccentric move, demolished his property's stables in order to turn them into an art gallery.

Horbury Crescent
NOTTING HILL GATE, W11

Until the nineteenth century, Notting Hill consisted of fields and rolling hills, owned by the Ladbroke Estate. This elegant crescent of houses looks back to a time when James Weller Ladbroke began to develop pockets of his property for housing. Alongside fine houses, such as those pictured here, grew up areas of notorious slums, and Notting Hill began life as the diverse mixture of dwellings it remains to this day.

In the mid-nineteenth century, around the same time as Horbury Crescent was being built, the Ladbroke family also attempted to turn a plot of nearby land into a racecourse. The Hippodrome opened to the public in 1837, but the heavy-going soil proved too difficult for the horses, and owners began to pull their animals out of the races. The course failed after just four years and the encompassing land was turned into a residential area.

'Notting Hill Gate' refers to a turnpike gate, built in the 1700s for traffic arriving in London from the West of England. Not far away is the magnificent Kensal Green cemetery, modelled on Paris's Père Lachaise cemetery. Many famous people are buried at Kensal Green, including William Thackeray, Wilkie Collins, Anthony Trollope and Isambard Kingdom Brunel.

Covent Garden Market
WC2

*Covent Garden Market at sunrise too, in the spring or summer,
when the fragrance of sweet flowers is in the air, overpowering even the
unwholesome streams of last night's debauchery, and driving the dusky thrush,
whose cage has hung outside a garrett window all night half mad with joy!*
The Old Curiosity Shop, *Charles Dickens, 1841*

The name 'Covent Garden' harks back to medieval times when this area was a convent garden, supplying the table of Westminster Abbey. The land was appropriated by the Crown after the Dissolution of the Monasteries and presented to the first Earl of Bedford. His descendant, Francis Russell, decided to develop the land, for which he employed the master architect, Inigo Jones. Influenced greatly by the Italian style, Jones laid out what is now Covent Garden's Piazza – London's first square.

In keeping with Covent Garden's origins, a famous fruit and vegetable market started here in the seventeenth century. In 1974, the market finally moved away (it is now at Nine Elms, SW8) and a fabulous reconstruction took place, the results of which can be seen here. Today it is a market of a different kind, with a profusion of shops, craft stalls and a wonderful variety of places to eat and drink.

Jack Straw's Castle
HAMPSTEAD, NW3

The original inn that stood on this site was a popular coaching inn for those passengers requiring respite before continuing their journey, or for those wary of travelling over Hampstead Heath at night for fear of highwaymen.

Jack Straw was one of the leaders of the Peasants' Revolt of 1381. It is said that he hid on this site after the riots – but he was eventually captured by the authorities and executed. The Peasants' Revolt resulted from a century of unrest due to exorbitant taxes, in particular the excessively corrupt poll-tax. To a population already decimated and traumatised by the first outbreak of the bubonic plague, the unrealistic taxes were doubly crippling.

The overall leader of the rebels was Wat Tyler, an ex-soldier. He rallied his new troops for a protest march on London and two groups set off, one from Kent and one from Essex, to petition the king. Unfortunately the frenzied mob began looting even before they left their own counties and by the time they reached London were at fever pitch. The revolt ended in full-scale rioting and the leaders were executed without being able to talk to the king. Ironically, the 14-year-old Richard II was sympathetic to their cause.

Kynance Mews
SW7

Mews streets are pleasant, quiet streets tucked away behind rows of grander houses all over London. Mews houses are developed from the myriad of old stables that once stood behind all expensive town houses.

The stables were essential in the time before motor vehicles and were usually accompanied by a carriage house. As well as housing horses, mews were often the home of the household's other animals, such as birds of prey used for hunting. The animals' carers were also housed in this part of the household and the mews had a community life of their own. Church services were even occasionally held there to accommodate all those who worked in the mews. Today houses such as those seen here are widely sought after and can command disproportionately high prices.

This particular mews street is comfortably situated in the exclusive area of Kensington; within walking distance of the wonderful shopping opportunities of Kensington High Street, the elegance of Gloucester Road and the museums that line Cromwell Road.

Oxford Street
W1

Oxford Street runs from Marble Arch, at the edge of Hyde Park, to the intersection with Tottenham Court Road and Charing Cross Road, known as St Giles's Circus. The street is London's most popular shopping street and home to some of retail's most famous names, including Selfridges, Marks and Spencers, John Lewis and Debenhams.

It takes its name from the time that the road, as part of an ancient Roman-road system, formed a major section of the route from London to Oxford. In the early eighteenth century, houses, theatres and inns began to be built along its boundaries and it became a residential area, popular for its proximity to the royal parks. It was not until the end of the nineteenth century that Oxford Street began to accommodate shops.

Today millions of people from all over the world visit the stores of Oxford Street and, during the January and summer sales, the pavements regularly become gridlocked with shoppers all attempting to find the best bargains. At Christmas the street is adorned with a legendary display of lights. Each year, these are switched on by a celebrity and large crowds gather to watch.

The National Gallery
TRAFALGAR SQUARE, WC2

The idea of a National Gallery was put forward in 1824 when the government purchased 38 works of art as a gift to the nation. The original building, designed by Willie Wilkins, was finished in 1838 and, after 14 years, the nation's pictures were brought to their new home. Until then, they had been stored in a private house.

In 1991, a new part of the Gallery, the Sainsbury Wing, was opened. When the project was first announced, several architects submitted very modern proposals of how the new building should look. These famously incurred the anger of Prince Charles and, for a while, the press had a field day reporting the heir to the throne's scathing comments about modern British architecture. Today the completed wing blends innocuously with Wilkins's grand Neo-Classical design.

The National Gallery is just one of several magnificent buildings which adorn Trafalgar Square, but it is one of the most beautiful. Its sheer size makes the panoramic view of the gallery breathtaking. Just around the corner stands the National Portrait Gallery, which opened in 1895. Between them, the two galleries house well over 10,000 exhibits.

Portobello Road Market
PORTOBELLO ROAD, W11

The market held at Portobello Road, situated close to the trendy areas of Notting Hill Gate and Ladbroke Grove, is a mecca for people searching for unique clothing and jewellery, as well as a popular haunt of tourists seeking souvenirs and antiques.

The first market stalls were set up at Portobello Road in the first half of the nineteenth century; the market then was mainly a place to buy fruit, vegetables and herbs. Today the market's stallholders offer clothes, antiques and arts and crafts alongside the fruit and vegetables. In fact Portobello Road market has grown to such an extent that it is now the world's largest outdoor antique market – a tradition that started after the Second World War, when the Caledonian antiques market, in Caledonian Road, closed down.

Portobello Road is home to market stalls every day of the week, except Sundays. As well as the wealth of things to buy, the market is also a fantastic place to visit for its great atmosphere, enlivened by the omnipresent street performers and the many culinary delights on offer.

Tailor's Window
CHANCERY LANE, WC2

The name of Ede and Ravenscroft has been associated with fine tailoring since 1689. Although the Season is more muted than it was in the eighteenth and nineteenth centuries, it still exists. Royal Ascot, Henley and debutantes' balls still take place annually and tailors such as Ede and Ravenscroft supply Society with its required trappings.

Chancery Lane is actually a corruption of 'Chancellors Lane', the name the street was known by in the fourteenth century. Cardinal Wolsey is believed to have lived here as did the seventeenth-century author Isaak Walton (who wrote *The Compleat Angler*).

North of Chancery Lane is Holborn, the area around which has been home to Francis Bacon, John Milton and Charles Dickens. Many of Dickens's characters have associations with the Holborn area and it was while living in the vicinity that Dickens first found fame with *The Pickwick Papers*. The name 'Holborn' comes from the Holebourne tributary; just as Fleet Street is named after the Fleet river.

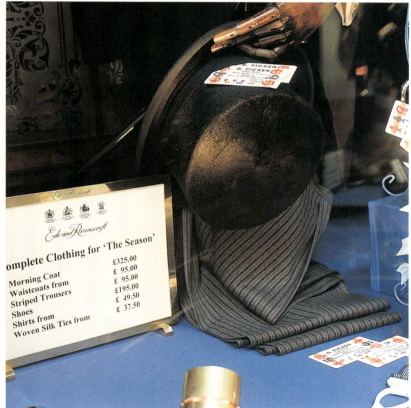

The Tate Gallery
PIMLICO, SW1

The Tate Gallery was bequeathed to the nation by Sir Henry Tate; he paid for its construction and donated his own collection of nineteenth-century British art. It opened in 1897, as the National Gallery of British Art, displaying works by artists born after 1790.

The building, designed by Sidney J. R. Smith, was constructed on the site of an old prison, the Millbank Penitentiary, which had been pulled down in 1892. In 1910, 1926 and 1937, the Gallery was added to under the patronage of the aristocratic Duveen family. Further building work took place in 1979 and 1987. Since then, Tate Galleries have been opened in St Ives, Cornwall, and in Liverpool.

Today the Tate houses some of the world's best modern art, by names such as Stubbs, Picasso, Rodin, Lichtenstein and Sickert. In 2000, the new Tate Gallery of Modern Art will open in the converted Bankside Power Station and, in 2001, the gallery here will be reopened as the Tate Gallery of British Art, housing works from 1500 to the present. This will provide public access to a much larger collection of the Tate's acquisitions (the greatest collection of British art in the world) than can be viewed currently. It will also allow the museum to revert to the original philosophy of Sir Henry Tate.

Tube Station
TOTTENHAM COURT ROAD, W1

London's underground train system is fondly known as 'the Tube'. It is the world's oldest underground railway and covers a massive area, reaching to the far outskirts of the city in all directions.

The first tube line to start up was the Metropolitan line; it ran from Amersham (in Buckinghamshire) to Whitechapel (not far from the Tower of London) and was opened in 1863. The first workable section of this line ran between Paddington and King's Cross. Today there are 11 tube lines as well as the connecting Docklands Light Railway.

Tottenham Court Road is a bustling station that provides access to the shopping mecca of Oxford Street and the myriad streets around St Giles's Circus. In previous centuries, however, this was a rural area encompassing a manor house, Tottenham Court, and Tottenham Fields. The road itself was the access route to the manor from the residential area of Oxford Street. There was also a brewery, which stood on the site of the present-day Dominion Theatre, and a seventeenth-century pub. Nowadays, Tottenham Court Road is perhaps best known for its plethora of electrical shops.

Victoria Station
VICTORIA, SW1

Victoria Station opened on 1 October 1860. When first built, it occupied 14 acres of land; there was no grand building on the site at this time – the cost of the tracks and engine sheds had left only enough capital to erect several temporary wooden shacks to house the passengers and station staff.

In 1868, the station expanded to house an underground railway station and in 1892, further land was purchased, including the Grosvenor Hotel, which was rebuilt in the Renaissance style. In 1911, Victoria also housed the first Post Office to be built within a London railway station.

The station became London's main gateway to the Continent and during the First World War was a pivotal centre for troops travelling to and from France. During the Second World War, Victoria was hit several times: at one point a German bomber crashed into the station.

Between the wars, Victoria entered the golden age of Continental travel whisking well-heeled holidaymakers away on the luxury boat-trains to Europe and on the Flying Boat services that connected Britain with the rest of the world. Victoria has continued its strong links with air and boat travel and today one can still see travellers – whether with backpacks or sets of designer luggage – wending their way through Victoria Station.

Well Tavern

HAMPSTEAD, NW3

I like to write when I feel spiteful; it's like having a good sneeze.

D. H. Lawrence in a letter to Lady Cynthia Asquith

The Well Tavern, situated on Well Walk, harks back to a time when Hampstead was famous as a spa town. During the early years of the eighteenth century, this area of London revelled in its newly found fortune as an area for wealthy invalids to visit and convalesce, however it soon became discredited due to its equal attraction for gamblers and those seeking the thrills of illicit rendezvous. The Well Tavern itself was a popular place for couples to meet and stay, and it gained a clandestine reputation.

During the nineteenth century, the surrounding area once again became fashionable.

Its many famous residents included John Constable, J. B. Priestly, D. H. Lawrence and John Keats. The poet came here with his consumptive brother, Tom, whom he nursed devotedly. Sadly the spa's healing waters were of no avail, nor did they protect John from contracting the disease.

New Scotland Yard
SW1

New Scotland Yard is the headquarters of the Metropolitan Police. The offices take their unusual name from their original location within Whitehall Palace. The area of the palace that Robert Peel's first police officers operated from was formerly the lodging allotted to Kings of Scotland, hence it became known as Great Scotland Yard. Eventually, the 'Great' was dropped and the name Scotland Yard became synonymous with the police, losing all earlier associations with Scottish royalty.

In 1890, the headquarters moved to new buildings sited close to Westminster Bridge – a move enforced by a Fenian bomb that had exploded in the Whitehall offices. It was at this time that the name New Scotland Yard came into general usage.

In the 1960s, the offices of New Scotland Yard moved to Broadway and Victoria Street; ironically near to the former lodgings of Dick Turpin. The infamous highwayman, now almost a figure of fable, lived during the eighteenth century. He and his horse, Black Bess, were the terror of London society for many years, particularly around Hampstead Heath, where he frequently waylaid coaches on their way into town.

The RITZ
PICCADILLY, W1

César Ritz, the son of a Swiss shepherd, was born in 1850. While still in his teens, Ritz worked his way through a variety of kitchens and restaurants; by his seventeenth birthday he had arrived in Paris. Here he worked at Voisin, one of the city's most fashionable restaurants, where he remained throughout the Franco-Prussian War – during the siege of Paris, Ritz found himself serving alien dishes such as elephant trunk (from animals of the former royal menagerie) and rat meat.

After the war, Ritz began working his way around the world of European tourism, becoming the favoured waiter of the Prince of Wales (later Edward VII). Around this time, Ritz also made the acquaintance of the great chef Auguste Escoffier and together they forged an unbeatable partnership. When the celebrated duo moved to Richard D'Oyly Carte's new London hotel, the Savoy, they brought an influential, rich clientele.

Ritz and Escoffier left the Savoy in 1894. Their perfectionist ideals of how their own hotel should be run became the backbone of the London Ritz, designed by Charles Mewes and Arthur J. Davies. Sadly, César died in 1918, just a few years after the completion of the hotel. It remains, however, a monument to his lifelong ambition and one of London's most illustrious institutions.

MAGNIFICENT ARCHITECTURE

From the elegant Regency lines of Park Crescent and the Gothic splendour of St Pancras Station, to the well-loved silhouette of Battersea's Art Deco Power Station, London's architecture is always dramatic, varied and awe-inspiring.

Park Crescent
W1

Park Crescent is a splendid example of the work of John Nash (1752-1835), one of the most prominent architects of the early nineteenth century, whose works also include Regent's Street and Buckingham Palace. This spectacular sweeping crescent was originally designed as a full circle, but the developer went bankrupt when it was less than half finished. Later developers decided only to complete the first semi-circle, and that is how it has remained. Today the façade is all that remains of Nash's work – the interiors were converted, mainly into offices, in the 1960s.

Park Crescent is named after what was Marylebone Park, today called Regent's Park (after George, the Prince Regent). Nash also landscaped the park into the desirable form it retains to this day. Together with its surrounding area, it included Regent's Canal, elegant shopping arcades, a botanical garden and a boating lake. Regent's Park is also home to London Zoo and residents often wake up to the sound of a lion roaring through the mist of an early morning.

Big·Ben
WESTMINSTER, SW1

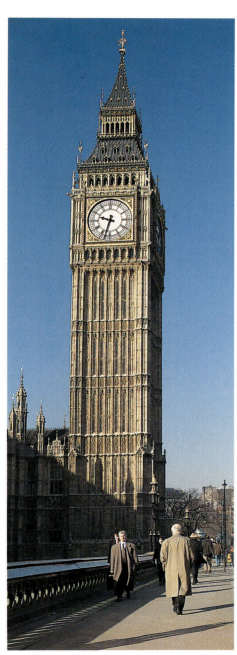

Big Ben is an integral part of British life. The sound of its chimes announced the end of the First World War and, in 1923, the tradition was begun of broadcasting to the nation the sound of Big Ben striking midnight on 31 December.

The name 'Big Ben' actually refers to the 13-ton bell; the clock tower is called St Stephen's tower. The structure in its entirety measures 314 ft tall and was designed by Sir Charles Barry as part of the reconstructed Palace of Westminster, which houses Parliament. He completed this project in 1854.

The bell one hears today is the second bell; the first (which weighed 16 tons) cracked in half in October 1857, just 14 months after being cast. It was melted down and made into the second bell; this also has a slight crack, but nevertheless continues to toll unimpeded.

The four richly ornate clock faces measure 23 feet in diameter. Each face contains 312 separate glass components, each minute space measures one square foot and the minute hands are 14 feet long. The hour hands are nine feet in length. Inscribed in gold lettering beneath each face is a Latin inscription, *Domine salvam fac reginam nostram Victoriam primam*, which translates as 'O Lord, save our Queen Victoria the First'.

Burgh House
HAMPSTEAD, NW3

Burgh House was built in 1703 in Queen Anne style. When the surrounding area became renowned for its medicinal waters, Burgh House was home to Dr William Gibbons, the physician who had made the discovery. He was appointed chief spa doctor and was reponsible for adding most of the architecture seen today. In later years the area became a barracks for the Royal East Middlesex militia, with the house serving as the Headquarters and Officers' Mess.

In 1884, the house passed once more into domestic ownership and, in 1908, the famous landscape gardener Gertrude Jekyll was asked to design the parkland around the house; sadly little of her work remains in evidence today.

From 1934-37 Rudyard Kipling's daughter, Elsie, lived here with her husband, Captain George Bambridge. The last journey from home that Rudyard Kipling made before his death was to Burgh House.

After the Second World War, the house's fortunes suffered a downward turn and the council, who were the current owners, threatened to close it. A local appeal ensured its survival and today the house is open to visitors. It also houses the Hampstead Museum.

Canary Wharf
DOCKLANDS, E14

London's docklands, which were so active in earlier centuries, became largely disused in the twentieth century when railways, cars and air travel largely replaced the need for transportation of goods by water. After several decades of falling into disrepair, the area was given a new lease of life in 1991 with the opening of the Canary Wharf complex. Since then numerous companies have moved their offices into the area and it has become one of the business world's most prestigious addresses.

Canary Wharf covers an area of 71 acres. Its most distinctive feature is Canada Tower, Europe's tallest office block and the UK's tallest building. The magnificent tower was designed by the architect Cesar Pelli. From its top floor, one can see for miles: looking to the west one can see the royal residence of Windsor Castle in the county of Berkshire and, to the east, Canvey Island in the county of Essex, can be seen.

Channel Four Building
HORSEFERRY ROAD, SW1

This stunning building was designed by the Richard Rogers Partnership – the architects of the Lloyd's Building. It was built between 1991 and 1994. When Richard Rogers took on the site, there was a 10 m-deep basement already, from an earlier abandoned project; this is now the site of Channel 4's main studio space.

This building is only part of the site owned by the television company, which encloses Channel 4's offices alongside proposed residential areas. The office building itself is composed of two wings, set in an L-shape, connected by the sweeping curve seen in this photograph. The pillar at the left side of the curved entrance houses four conference rooms, sited on four levels; the pillar to the right-hand side contains the lifts.

The frame of the construction was composed of concrete, on top of which was laid powder-coated aluminium, giving it the distinctive and distinguished pewter-grey colour seen here. The architects were extremely mindful of the workers who would occupy this building, as well as those who would look upon it, and one of the many assets of these offices is a curved restaurant with views of the garden.

Royal Courts of Justice
THE STRAND, WC2

From 1873 to 1875, several bills were passed that would change the course of British legal history; namely the Judicature Acts. Their aim was to centralise the legal system, thereby outlawing the many 'specialist' courts that had sprung up throughout England and Wales, all of which dealt with a different type of crime. The problems caused by these courts were that justice was becoming apportioned into disparate sections and the individual courts were becoming laws unto themselves. The Judicature Acts paved the way for a Supreme Court of Judicature.

The Royal Courts of Justice were the result of these legal proceedings and, after a fiercely fought competition, the chosen architect was George Edmund Street, R. A. Building work began according to his designs in 1873, but sadly Street died before seeing his plans completed. Due to a stonemason strike at the time, much of the labour that built the Royal Courts of Justice was imported, mainly from Germany. The workers' presence so enraged the strikers, that they were placed under police protection. The building was opened in 1882 in a ceremony performed by Queen Victoria.

Imperial War Museum
LAMBETH ROAD, SE1

The first Imperial War Museum was set up after the First World War, when it was housed at Crystal Palace. By 1936 it had moved to its present site. Poignantly, the building sustained air-raid damage during the Second World War, but this was soon repaired.

The building that houses the museum was actually the main section of the Bethlehem Royal Hospital, better known as 'Bedlam'. The history of this hospital for the insane dates back to 1247, although it was not moved to this site until 1815. Early conditions were barbaric and the hospital was infamous for the brutality of its methods of correction. Fortuitously, these began to change after the insanity of King George III became known: public attitude towards victims of insanity became more sympathetic, and conditions improved. However, despite this, it remained common practice for people to go and view the patients at Bedlam. Until the end of the nineteenth century it was a popular Sunday afternoon jaunt, viewed in the same way as going to the zoo.

After the First World War, the hospital was removed to Kent, where it still remains. The wings of the building had been badly damaged during the war, but the museum took over the main block.

Battersea Power Station
BATTERSEA, SW11

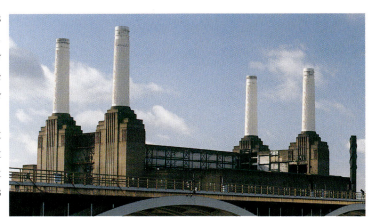

Battersea Power Station was designed by Sir Giles Gilbert Scott as the London Power Station. Construction began in 1929 and was complete by 1935. Gilbert Scott was responsible only for the exterior, the interior was elaborately designed by Halliday & Agate.

The distinctive building, with its four 337-feet high chimneys, initially caused great public outcry. It eventually became fêted as a superb example of Art Deco architecture, and today is one of London's most loved features.

In 1983, the Electricity Board, who owned the building, closed down their power plant. The building was sold on to a developer who intended

to turn it into an indoor theme park. However, this idea folded through lack of finances and the magnificent edifice remained empty. In 1993, a Hong Kong conglomerate bought the site and some adjoining land, with the intention of turning it into a vast leisure complex. The proposed plans included a 30-screen cinema, offices, two hotels with conference facilities, residential apartments, a post-production film studio, theatres, shops and a new railway station. Thankfully, as the power station was awarded Grade II listed status in 1980, whatever the developers choose to do with it, the façade has to remain the same.

Michelin Building
FULHAM ROAD, SW3

The Michelin Building, in South Kensington, is one of the finest, and most colourful, examples of Art Nouveau design in England. It was designed by Epinasse and took two years to complete, opening in 1911. Originally a garage for the French Michelin Company, today the building has become one of London's most exclusive business addresses. It houses several companies, smart eateries and expensive shops.

Art Nouveau originated in central Europe at the end of the nineteenth century. Examples of early Art Nouveau structures include the church of Saint-Jean L'Evangeliste at Montmartre and many of the Paris Métro stations, designed by Hector Guimard. In England, the Arts and Crafts movement was in full throttle at the time that Art Nouveau was catching on in France, Germany, Italy, Austria and Spain, so it is unsurprising that the French Michelin company was the first to build a recognisably Art Nouveau structure in London.

Natural History Museum
SOUTH KENSINGTON, SW7

Originally, London's natural history exhibits could be found in the British Museum in Bloomsbury. In 1860, it was decided that a new, separate building was required to house the ever-increasing specimens – this was the age of exploration and discovery and natural scientists of every discipline were constantly unearthing new finds.

The Natural History Museum, designed by Alfred Waterhouse, was unveiled in 1881. Its many-coloured terracotta exterior, built on a framework of iron and steel, has earned it deserved recognition as one of the most beautiful buildings in London. Parts of the museum were battered by bombs in the Second World War and complementary additions were made in 1959, 1963 and 1977.

The interiors are equally as stunning as the exterior, incorporating sweeping arches, ornamented colonnades and lavish decorations of plants and animals. This wealth of architectural excellence has led to the museum being in great demand for private functions and, on many occasions, guests at exclusive parties or balls have the pleasure of drinking, eating and dancing beneath the watchful skeleton of the museum's diplodocus.

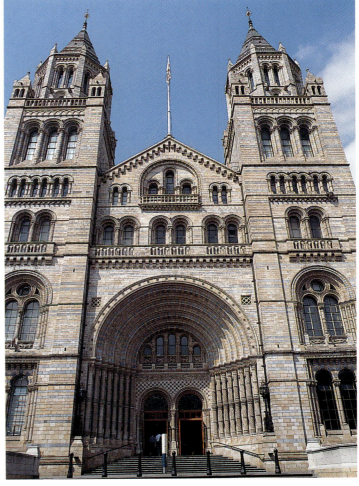

Paddington Station
W2

The original Paddington Station was a temporary wooden construction that opened in 1838. The present building, designed by Isambard Kingdom Brunel (1806-59), was unveiled in 1854. Much of the internal decoration, such as the wrought-iron roof seen here, was created by the architect M. D. Wyatt, but the bulk of the station's design was realised by Brunel. The master engineer was greatly inspired by the contemporary Crystal Palace (designed by Joseph Paxton), and Paddington Station, together with the adjoining Great Western Royal Hotel, became one of Victorian London's most elegant landmarks. A statue of Brunel takes pride of place in the station.

In 1958, the name of Paddington became even more famous, with the publication of Michael Bond's magical children's books about Paddington Bear. Bond's hero is a small Peruvian bear who is sent to England, with only a suitcase and a label asking someone to take care of him. He is discovered at Paddington Station by the Brown family, who adopt him and name him after the place he was found. Today the station still houses a Paddington Bear stall, selling mementoes of the small bear whose name is associated with this place throughout the world.

Marble Arch
W1

Marble Arch was originally part of John Nash's remodelled Buckingham Palace. The triumphal arch (celebrating the victorious battles of Trafalgar and Waterloo) was built in 1827 as part of an open courtyard in the Palace grounds.

Nash's one oversight was the width of the arch – it was too narrow to allow a carriage to pass through. That defect, coupled with Queen Victoria's desire to extend the Palace in order to accommodate more nurseries, led to Marble Arch being moved. In 1851, it was uprooted and taken to the north-east corner of Hyde Park, where it remains today.

At the beginning of the twentieth century the area around the arch was separated from the main body of Hyde Park, and today the proud symbol of victory stands at the centre of one of the busiest road systems in London. Few of the millions of people who walk or drive around this area today are aware of the site's history as a place of public execution. Where Marble Arch stands was once called Tyburn, and it was here that the gallows swung. Beneath the gallows, and consequently beneath the arch, are buried the bodies of Oliver Cromwell and two of his men.

Royal Opera Arcade
SW1

The Royal Opera Arcade runs between Pall Mall and Charles II Street. Confusingly, its name does not arise from the Royal Opera House in Covent Garden; instead it comes from the former Haymarket Opera House, now known as Her Majesty's Theatre, to which the arcade is attached.

There has been a theatre here since the very beginning of the eighteenth century. Unfortunately, the original, extravagant building was destroyed by fire in 1783. By this time, it had gained a strong reputation both for its plays and as the birthplace of many of Handel's operas, so a replacement was erected in the 1790s. The new building was designated an opera house and began life as one of London's most popular venues – sadly this was all to change with the competition afforded by its Covent Garden rival. In the 1890s, the theatre was knocked down; the only remaining part of it being the Royal Opera Arcade.

Her Majesty's Theatre was built just before the turn of the century. Its designer was C. J. Phipps, who took his inspiration from the architecture of the French Renaissance. A few years later the Royal Academy of Dramatic Arts (known as RADA) was set up alongside the new theatre; it was later moved to Gower Street, WC1.

Senate House
UNIVERSITY COLLEGE LONDON, WC1

The University's Senate House was opened in 1936 to a public outcry – at that time the general consensus was that architecture should conform to a classical style and Charles Holden's design was felt to be garishly modern. The impressive tower, which stands at 210 ft high, dominates the area around Malet Street in which it stands, and today it is viewed as one of the best examples of Art Deco architecture in London.

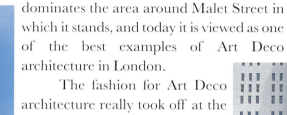

The fashion for Art Deco architecture really took off at the end of the 1920s. In 1925, the *Exposition Internationale des Arts Décoratif et Industriels Modernes* was held in Paris. It was from this that 'Art Deco' gained its name. By the 1930s the movement had taken hold throughout Western Europe and America and many of London's buildings of that era, such as the Hoover Building on the Great West Road and BBC Radio's Broadcasting House in Portland Place, were modelled in this style; as were the Chrysler and Empire State Buildings in New York.

The University itself was opened in 1828. At that time it was almost impossible to go to university unless one was a member of the Church of England. The University of London (as it was then called) was the first university to offer an exceptional education to those of all denominations.

Southwark Cathedral
SOUTHWARK, SE1

In Southwark at the Tabard as I lay
Ready to go on my pilgrimage to Canterbury
At night there came into that hostelry
Some nine and twenty in a company.

'The Prologue' *from* **The Canterbury Tales,**
Geoffrey Chaucer, 1387

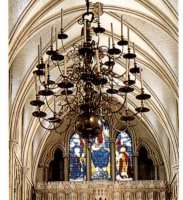

Southwark Cathedral has one of the longest histories of any building in London – there has been a church on this site since the ninth century. The original building was elaborately restored in the fifteenth century and then again in the late-nineteenth century. However, much of the architecture dates back many centuries and extremely ancient tombs are to be found within its walls. William Shakespeare's brother, Edmund, is buried here, as are the Jacobean playwrights John Fletcher and Philip Massinger.

Stories of the cathedral's origins differ, but it appears to have been founded by one of two people: a woman called Mary, daughter of the ferryman who took passengers across the Thames at Southwark, or St Swithin, Bishop of Winchester, who died in AD 862. His feast day is celebrated on the 15 July, but he is chiefly remembered for an ancient saying, of unknown origin, that declares whatever the weather is on his feast day, it will remain so for the following 40 days.

St Pancras Station

EUSTON ROAD, NW1

St Pancras was a fourteen-year-old Christian boy, who was martyred in Rome in AD 304 by the Emperor Diocletian. In England he is better known as a railway station.
'St Pancras', *Sir John Betjeman*

St Pancras railway station was one of the crowning glories of nineteenth-century English architecture. The station, designed by William Henry Barlow, was constructed from 60 million bricks, 9,000 tons of steel and iron and 14 different types of stone. It took 6,000 men, 1,000 horses and 100 steam-operated cranes four years to build. The adjoining hotel was designed by George Gilbert Scott and contained 400 bedrooms. It was opened in 1873.

The station's railway lines were constructed on the site of the old St Pancras Chapel's burial ground. The work, directed by A. W. Blomfield, began in 1866 and a public outcry ensued, fanned by reports of passers-by glimpsing bones, skulls and, in one instance, a shining head of hair protruding from an upset grave. The reburials that ensued were overseen by Blomfield's assistant – the young Thomas Hardy. Afterwards, he wrote two poems about the experience.

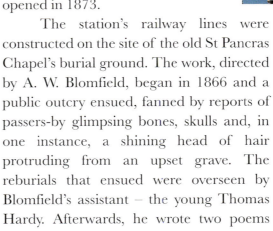

Trinity House
TRINITY SQUARE, EC3

In 1514, Henry VIII agreed a Royal Charter to create a Guild of Shipmen and Mariners of England; today that corporation has become the General Lighthouse Authority for England, Wales and the Channel Islands. Its headquarters are at Trinity House, from which the corporation oversees the administration of charitable funds in connection with sailors and all those who go to sea. After the death of Henry VIII, the corporation continued to receive Royal patronage. Their Charter was renewed both by Mary I and Elizabeth I, ensuring the continuation of the tradition.

The corporation's first lighthouse was at Lowestoft; built in 1609. The authorities of Trinity House were also responsible for most other maritime features, such as beacons, buoys and official ship documentation. The corporation was also the only authority allowed to issue licences to boats wishing to use the Thames.

The first Trinity House was in Deptford (where Henry had his Royal Docks), but by the 1660s, the corporation had been relocated to the area of London in which the present building stands. In 1666, Trinity House was destroyed in the Great Fire of London, but was rebuilt on the same site.

Victoria & Albert Museum
CROMWELL ROAD, SW7

After the success of the Great Exhibition of 1851, the organisers purchased a large area of land in South Kensington. Their intention was to erect museums in order to continue the education of the nation. In 1857, the first building of what is now the Victoria & Albert Museum was completed; by all accounts it was an ugly, iron-clad building. The museum was opened officially by Queen Victoria on 22 June 1857. Visitors could view a wealth of fine paintings, sculptures, textiles: all superior works of art. In 1884 the museum presented the National Art Library to the nation. It remains one of England's premier art libraries to this day.

In 1899, two years before her death, Queen Victoria laid the foundation stone of a new building to be erected on the same site as the original building, which had been removed to Bethnal Green. The new museum was completed in 1909 and given its current name in memory of the deceased royal couple.

Since that time, additional work has constantly taken place at the museum. The most recent feature, the Pirelli Garden, was added in 1987. It is an oasis of greenery set amid an Italianate courtyard.

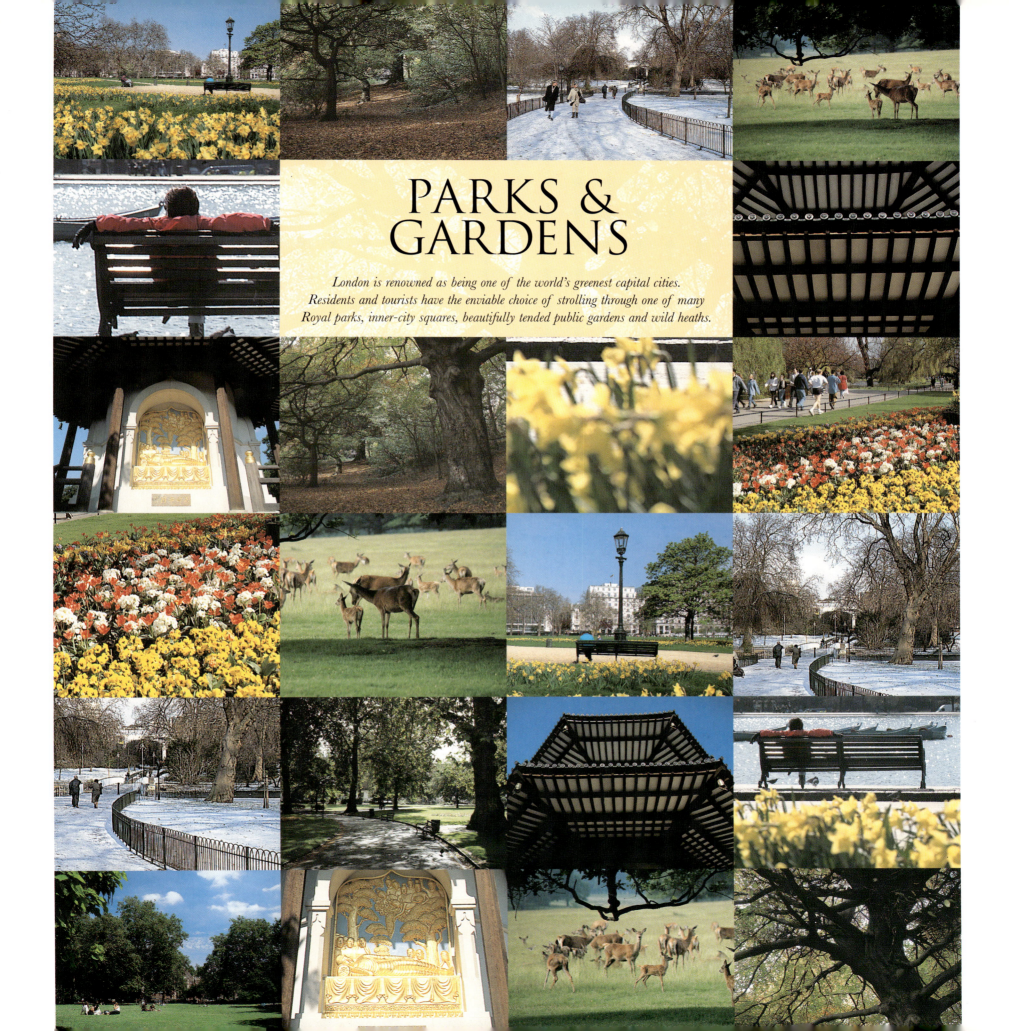

PARKS & GARDENS

London is renowned as being one of the world's greenest capital cities. Residents and tourists have the enviable choice of strolling through one of many Royal parks, inner-city squares, beautifully tended public gardens and wild heaths.

St James's Park
ST JAMES'S, SW1

Of all the sights in London, there is one that is certain to astonish all first-time visitors – the sight of pelicans floating unconcernedly on the water at St James's Park. Exotic birds, including pelicans, were first introduced to the park during the reign of King Charles II. In 1603, the park had been newly landscaped for King James I; these new designs included a duck pond. In 1667, the ducks were superseded by their more exotic relations. The pelicans have remained ever since.

St James's Park was first appropriated for royal use by Henry VIII; he laid claim to it in 1531 which makes it the oldest royal park in London. Since that time its design has changed several times, from formal to informal layouts, as has its royal owner. It was finally handed over to the people in the eighteenth century.

The park, which borders Buckingham Palace, is named after a hospital for the treatment of leprosy – St James's Hospital later became the illustrious St James's Palace.

Hampstead Heath
NW3

In the Middle Ages, wolves wandered across the area now known as Hampstead Heath. For many centuries, this was a rough place of wild open forest – until the town of Hampstead became fashionable as a spa resort. From that time onwards, the 'civilisation' of the heath became ever more pronounced and in 1906 it was presented to the public as a park. Today it is one of the most fascinating parks in London, encompassing 800 acres (3 sq miles) which include swimming ponds, woods (remnants of the old forest), a horse-riding area, fishing ponds, sports fields, lakes and, on Bank Holiday weekends, a funfair.

In the late-nineteenth century, the park's boundaries were extended to encompass the adjacent Parliament Hill, reputedly created from the burial mound of Boudicca – although no evidence has been found to support this claim. The hill's connection with 'parliament' is uncertain, although it has been suggested that it was the site where Guy Fawkes and his colleagues met to discuss their plan to blow up the Houses of Parliament.

Hyde Park
W1, W2 & SW7

He got up and looked out of the window...
In the flickering green of the square below some children were
flitting about like white butterflies, and the pavement was
crowded with people on their way to the Park.

Lord Arthur Savile's Crime, *Oscar Wilde, 1887*

In the seventeenth century, James I opened Hyde Park to the public and it rapidly became *the* place to be seen. Rotten Row – the name derives from Route du Roi or 'Road of the King' – became the most fashionable road in London. Each day grand crested carriages could be seen there, with wealthy occupants leisurely taking the air between St James's Palace and Kensington Palace.

On Easter Sunday, the Row became a parade ground for those wanting to show off their carefully trimmed Easter Bonnets, and May Day would not have been complete without a visit to Hyde Park. One of the most popular pastimes, and one that endures today, is a boating trip on the Park's lake, the Serpentine. Others prefer just to sit back on one of the Park's many benches and watch the world go by.

Lincoln's Inn Fields
WC2

*And hard by Temple Bar, in Lincoln's Inn Hall, at the very heart of the fog,
sits the Lord High Chancellor in his High Court of Chancery.*

Bleak House, Charles Dickens

Lincoln's Inn Fields was once an area of common ground made up of two fields; today it has the distinction of being London's largest square and one of the city's oldest residential areas. However, before it became a place of fashionable residence, Lincoln's Inn Fields was also used as a public execution spot. Many supposed traitors were hanged here, including hundreds of Roman Catholics accused of treason, during the reign of Queen Elizabeth I, purely on the grounds of their faith.

Lincoln's Inn Fields lie close to the heart of London's legal profession; both the Temple (the centre of London's legal community) and the Royal Courts of Justice can be reached within a few minutes walk from the square. A great many chapters of Charles Dickens's novel *Bleak House* are set around the area of Lincoln's Inn Fields and nearby Chancery Lane. Dickens's close friend (and biographer) John Forster was a resident of the square and the novelist visited him here regularly.

Peace Pagoda
BATTERSEA PARK, SW11

The Peace Pagoda in Battersea Park was built by Nipponzan Myohoji Buddhist monks and nuns; it took almost a year to complete and was unveiled in 1985. The enticing monument, whose serenity and unexpectedness attracts visitors to the park to wander up its steps, is 100 ft tall.

Traditionally pagodas are found in countries with a high Buddhist population, such as China, India, Myanmar and Japan. They may be erected as a shrine, a memorial or as a tomb. The first known pagodas appeared in China in *c.* AD 550. The platform of Battersea's Peace Pagoda affords views over a quiet stretch of the Thames, as well as over the park.

Battersea Park is a 192-acre oasis, situated on the south side of the Thames. Until the mid-nineteenth century, this area comprised soggy fields, prone to regular flooding from the river; however an Act of Parliament in 1846 fated the marshy land to become a public park. Towards the end of the nineteenth century, Battersea Park became *the* place to ride bicycles (an activity that was banned in other parks); a hundred years later it remains equally popular with rollerbladers as well as cyclists.

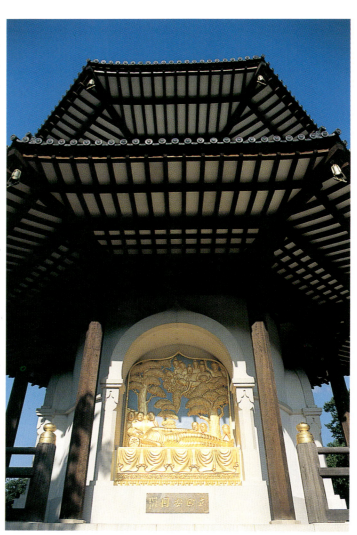

Regent's Park
NW1

Originally known as Marylebone Park, Regent's Park was formally laid out by John Nash following plans that were drawn up in 1811. Before it became a public park, Regent's Park was a Royal Park, used as a hunting ground. Before that time it was part of the estate of the Abbey of Tyburn, and previous to that was part of the enormous Forest of Middlesex, which encompassed swathes of what is now London.

During the Second World War, the park and its surrounding buildings, suffered fairly extensive bomb damage; however, all was lovingly restored over the ensuing years. The restoration was finally completed in the 1970s.

Regent's Park is one of the most idyllic places to spend a relaxing day. In summer, as well as the zoo, several magnificent bronze statues, the boating lake, beautifully landscaped gardens, picturesque walks and the much-used bandstand, there is the added attraction of the Open Air Theatre. During the, hopefully, clement months, lovers of Shakespeare can watch the Bard's plays performed as they would have been in Elizabethan times – under an open sky.

LONDON

Green Park
SW1

Green Park, one of London's Royal Parks, borders Hyde Park, St James's Park and Buckingham Palace Gardens. Originally a Royal hunting ground, the park was given to the public by Charles II in the seventeenth century.

During the eighteenth century, Green Park was often a dangerous place. It was a frequent haunt of highwaymen as well as a popular place for gentlemen to settle disagreements – with a duel. However, the park was also a renowned place of public entertainment and on occasions, such as Royal marriages or coronations, or in celebration of a national victory in battle, magnificent firework displays took place here. The park was also a popular spot for hot-air ballooning, a fashion that became popular in London in the latter half of the eighteenth century.

In the twentieth century, Green Park played an important part in the protection of Londoners. During the Second World War, provisions had to be made for those caught outside during air raids who would therefore be unable to make their way to their usual shelter. Green Park was one of several open spaces in London where trenches were built as communal shelters.

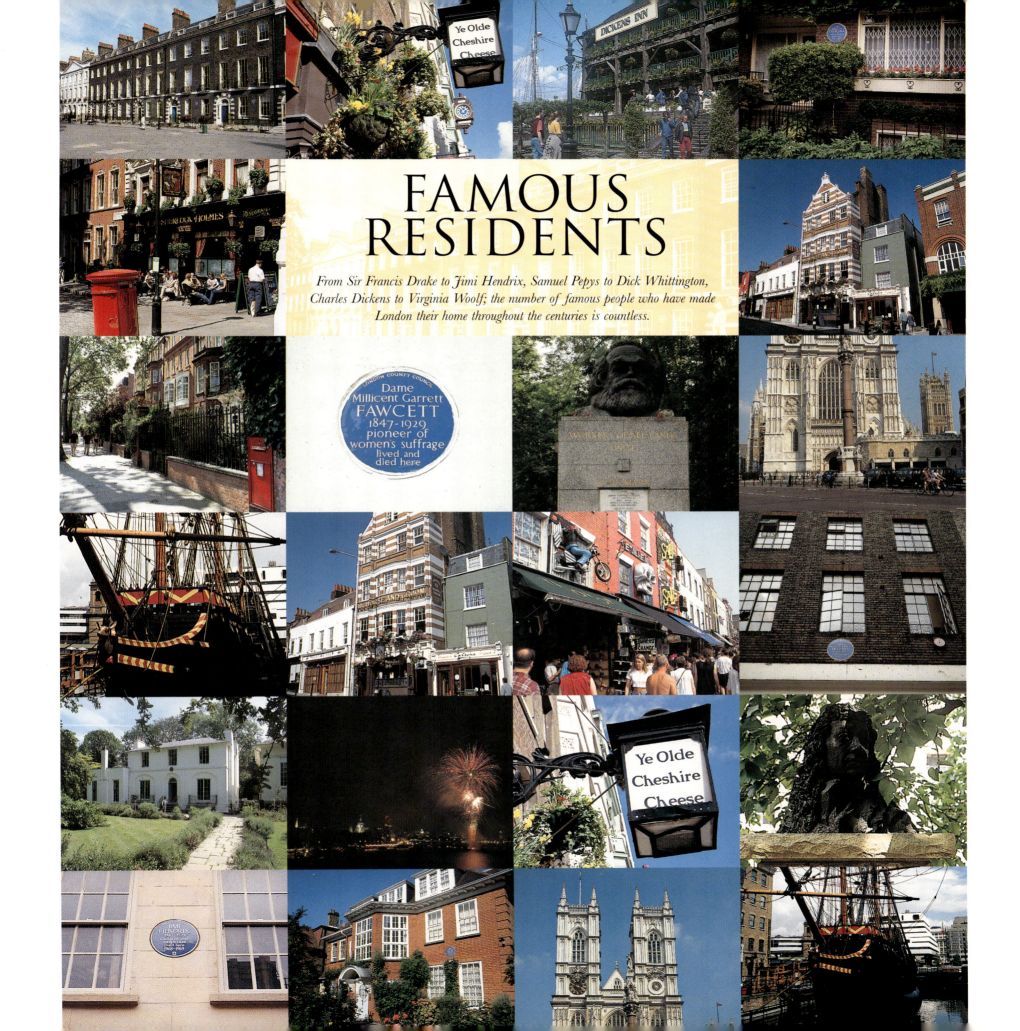

FAMOUS RESIDENTS

From Sir Francis Drake to Jimi Hendrix, Samuel Pepys to Dick Whittington,
Charles Dickens to Virginia Woolf; the number of famous people who have made
London their home throughout the centuries is countless.

Jimi Hendrix's Blue Plaque
W1

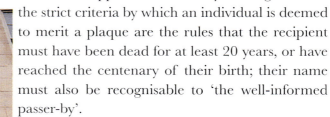

Blue plaques have become an essential feature of London. The first building to receive the decoration was Lord Byron's birthplace in Westminster, in 1867. Since that time an average of 18 plaques have been put up every year.

The awarding of plaques is organised by English Heritage, who receive hundreds of applications annually. Among  the strict criteria by which an individual is deemed to merit a plaque are the rules that the recipient must have been dead for at least 20 years, or have reached the centenary of their birth; their name must also be recognisable to 'the well-informed passer-by'.

Jimi Hendrix received his plaque in 1997. As a child, he played guitar in school bands, after which he became a paratrooper in the US Army. On leaving the army, he worked as a backing musician; at one point he played with Sam Cooke. When he attempted to go solo, Hendrix became frustrated at the unappreciative audience in his native America, so he left for England – here he became a megastar with his group, the Jimi Hendrix Experience. In 1967, he returned to America to play the legendary Monterey Pop Festival; two years later he was the closing act at Woodstock. Tragically, in September 1970, he died from a drugs overdose.

Bedford Square
BLOOMSBURY, WC1

... the carriages, motor cars, omnibuses, vans, sandwich men shuffling and swinging; brass bands; barrel organs; in the triumph and the jingle and the strange high singing of some aeroplane overhead was what she loved; life; London; this moment of June.
Mrs Dalloway, *Virginia Woolf, 1925*

Bedford Square is the only Bloomsbury square whose original Georgian architecture remains intact. Each front door has a patterned semicircular window above it, each one of which is patterned individually. This dates back to the time before house numbers were introduced: householders would have their own pattern printed on to the top of their invitations, writing paper and calling cards – visitors had simply to match up the pattern on their invitation to that on the front door.

Bloomsbury is best known for a resident group of writers, artists and free-thinking intellectuals who lived here in the late-nineteenth and early twentieth centuries. They became known as the Bloomsbury Group. This group included Virginia and Leonard Woolf, Vanessa and Clive Bell, John Lytton Strachey, Maynard Keynes, Roger Fry, Duncan Grant and David Garnett. This close-knit community also had ties with other names of note such as E. M. Forster, Dora Carrington and the society hostess Lady Otteline Morrell.

Camden High Street
CAMDEN, NW1

Camden was once a peaceful part of the countryside, replete with fields of cows, that was before the nineteenth-century arrival of London property developers. Within a few decades it had become a fashionable, respectable place to live, with easy access to the town and country.

Towards the end of the century, it had become less genteel and more bohemian and, by the early twentieth century, the Camden Town Group had come into existence. The nucleus of this important artistic clique was Walter Sickert, who set up the group together with 15 friends (including Augustus John and Wyndham Lewis). Much of the artists' work of this time can now be seen in London's finest art galleries, such as the Tate and the National Gallery.

Camden Town also has a secret side. Beneath the streets are a series of catacombs that run an extensive course. As well as the tunnels' usefulness for distributing goods between businesses without disturbing the public, they were also used to house ponies which worked in the warehouses and docks above ground. There is also a more grisly side to this area of London. Its name became a household phrase after the Camden Town Murders and, in 1843, the last fatal duel fought on British soil took place in a Camden field.

Cheyne Walk
CHELSEA, SW3 & SW10

Cheyne Walk, an exclusive residential area of Chelsea, has had an extraordinary number of famous residents. Those who have lived along this picturesque stretch of riverside London include the artists Dante Gabriel Rossetti, James McNeill Whistler, J. M. W. Turner and Sir Jacob Epstein; the writers George Eliot and Henry James – both of whom died here, the poet T. S. Eliot and the novelist Ian Fleming, creator of James Bond.

In the 1960s, Cheyne Walk was given a more modern famous perspective when Mick Jagger and Marianne Faithfull moved into Whistler's old house. Cheyne Walk remains one of London's most exclusive addresses and is visually distinctive for its plethora of blue plaques. It is popular for its proximity to the King's Road, one of London's most popular shopping streets and legendary in the world of fashion. It was here that Malcolm Maclaren, Mary Quant and Vivienne Westwood opened up boutiques in the Sixties and Seventies.

Today the road alongside Cheyne Walk's houses is part of one of London's busiest stretches of road; in the time of Rossetti and Whistler the street was a quiet, picturesque river walk within easy reach of the city centre.

Samuel Pepys' Garden
SW1

Up to my office, whither by agreement Mr. Coventry came before the time of setting to confer about preparing an account of the extraordinary charge of the Navy since the King's coming. So by and by we sat, and so till noon. Then home to dinner.

Diary of Samuel Pepys, *7 February 1663*

S amuel Pepys was born in 1633. He lived in London all his life, except for his years at university in Cambridge. His first job was in the house of his cousin, the first Earl of Sandwich. From there he went on to become a clerk to the Navy Board and eventually Secretary to the Admiralty.

Pepys' name has become synonymous with the wonderfully observant diaries he kept for nine years. The diaries run from 1660 to 1669 and provide us with a great deal of the historical knowledge we have about London in the seventeenth century. Perhaps the most important aspect of his diaries is that they begin before the Great Fire of London in 1666 and therefore provide the reader with an account of how London looked then. Today, his original diaries are kept in the Pepys Library at Cambridge.

Sigmund Freud's House
HAMPSTEAD, NW3

The only unnatural sexual behaviour is none at all.
Sigmund Freud

Sigmund Freud lived at this house, 20 Maresfield Gardens, at the end of his life. In 1990 it became a museum devoted to the great psychoanalyst.

Freud was born in Moravia (now part of the former Czechoslovakia) on 6 May 1856; when he was three years old, his family moved to Vienna. Freud trained for the medical profession and studied in several European locations, before returning to Vienna and establishing his practice at Berggasse 19 – today the house is also a Freud museum. When the Nazis annexed Austria in 1937, Freud and his family suffered terrifying harassment from Hitler's SS and fled to England. They spent a few months living in Elsworthy Road before moving a few roads to this address.

Freud was already an old man when he escaped from the Nazis and he died in London just two years later. He was cremated at Golders Green crematorium.

In 1970, a bronze statue of Freud was unveiled by five of his great-grandchildren in Adelaide Road, Swiss Cottage, not far from the two places in which he lived. It was cast by the artist Oscar Nemon, from an original 1930s mould.

Heath Street

HAMPSTEAD, NW3

The drive through London seemed endless,
and by the time we had drawn clear again and were out beyond
Hampstead there was a sound in my head like the beating of a drum.
Rebecca, *Daphne du Maurier*

Hampstead has long been the haunt of artists, writers and actors. Heath Street itself, although part of an ancient road system, was mainly constructed in 1887–89 when the local council decided to improve the town's layout. Unfortunately, in so doing, many of the original adjoining alleyways and courtyards were razed to the ground.

Many famous people have lived or stayed within walking distance of Heath Street. Among them the painter George Romney, the poet John Keats, the author Robert Louis Stevenson, the landscape artist John Constable, the writer John Galsworthy and several generations of the family of the author Daphne du Maurier. Daphne is usually associated with the West Country, but she spent her childhood in Hampstead and it was here, among streets such as this one, that she grew up and developed her writing skills.

Sherlock Holmes Pub
NW1

Where there is no imagination there is no horror.

A Study in Scarlet, *Sir Arthur Conan Doyle*

Although a fictional resident, Sherlock Holmes is one of London's best-known characters. His name has become synonymous with detectives and has become even more famous than that of his inventor, Sir Arthur Conan Doyle.

Sherlock Holmes first appeared in 1887, in the short story *A Study in Scarlet*. The prolific Conan Doyle then went on to write over 50 more stories concerning the great detective.

In the stories, Sherlock Holmes lives at 221b Baker Street. Today '221b' (actually sandwiched between numbers 237 and 239) is a museum commemorating the work of the detective himself, his partner in sleuthing, Dr Watson, and Holmes's arch-enemy, Professor Moriarty.

This pub also contains a wealth of Holmes memorabilia, including an effigy of the great man reading *The Times*. The wonderfully eccentric detective is described as hawk-nosed, slender and prone to wearing a deerstalker hat. He lives on nervous energy, is an avid reader and plays the violin in order to fine-tune his mind; he also takes cocaine habitually. His method of deduction is based on scientific reasoning – the character is reputed to have been based on Conan Doyle's medical tutor, Dr Joseph Bell.

Keats' House

HAMPSTEAD, NW3

Happy is England! I could be content
To see no other verdure than its own;
To feel no other breezes than are blown
Through its tall woods with high romances blent ...

'Happy is England! I Could be Content', *John Keats*

Despite the brevity of his life, John Keats (1795–1821) has become one of England's most important Romantic poets. He lived in this house for two years of his life, from 1818-20. One of his most famous poems, 'Ode to a Nightingale', was composed in the garden here.

Both Keats' parents died before his sixteenth birthday, as a result John and his brother, Tom, were looked after by a guardian. John trained as a doctor at two of London's premier hospitals, Guy's and St Thomas's, however, he also discovered a passion for poetry. In 1816, he achieved two of his ambitions: he finished his surgeon's training and had his first poem published. From that time onwards, medicine was decidedly secondary in his life.

In 1818, Tom died of tuberculosis, an illness through which Keats had nursed him. In 1819, Keats proposed to Fanny Brawne, but tragically, before they could marry, Keats himself succumbed to tuberculosis. At the time of his death he was seeking convalescence in Italy and, as a result, his grave is in Rome.

Lord Mayor's Show
VIEWED FROM VICTORIA EMBANKMENT, WC2

The tradition of a Lord Mayor's Show dates back to the thirteenth century. Today it is a spectacular ceremony that takes place annually, on the second Saturday in November, to mark the accession of a new Lord Mayor of London. The grand procession makes its way from the fifteenth-century Guildhall through the City, past Mansion House (the Lord Mayor's official residence), to the Law Courts, returning along the Embankment. At the end of the day is a dazzling firework display over the Thames.

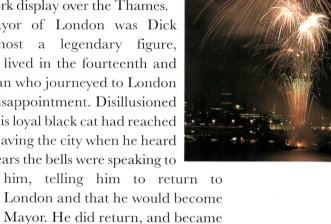

The most famous Lord Mayor of London was Dick Whittington. Although now almost a legendary figure, Whittington was a real person who lived in the fourteenth and fifteenth centuries. He was a poor man who journeyed to London to seek his fortune, but found only disappointment. Disillusioned and impoverished, Whittington and his loyal black cat had reached Highgate, and were on the point of leaving the city when he heard Bow Bells chiming. To Whittington's ears the bells were speaking to him, telling him to return to London and that he would become Mayor. He did return, and became Mayor – four times. Today a stone marks the spot from where Whittington heard the bells and a statue remembers his faithful cat.

The Dickens Inn
ST KATHARINE'S DOCK, E1

Charles John Huffam Dickens was born on 7 February 1812, one of eight children. After a settled early childhood, Charles's world was thrown into turmoil when his father, a government clerk, was imprisoned for debt. At the age of 12, Charles was forced into adulthood; spending miserable hours working in a blacking factory to support himself and his family. His entertainment at this time was the streets of London, where he spent many hours walking and meeting the characters that were later to people his novels.

A few years later, Charles gained employment as a reporter and began writing full time. While still in his early twenties, he became lauded as the author of *The Pickwick Papers*, rapidly becoming England's favourite novelist. His success is legendary and international, and he was responsible for such classic works of literature as *Oliver Twist*, *Great Expectations*, *Martin Chuzzlewit* and *A Tale of Two Cities*. Prolific in every aspect of his life, Charles

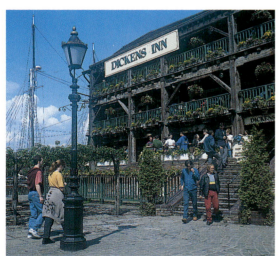

worked himself into an early grave. He died in 1870 at the age of 58, leaving his latest work, *The Mystery of Edwin Drood*, unfinished and a nation in mourning. Against his wishes – he wanted a quiet, family burial – Queen Victoria ordered a magnificent state funeral. After much ceremony, he was finally laid to rest in Poets' Corner, Westminster Abbey.

Grave of Karl Marx
EASTERN CEMETERY, HIGHGATE NW3

Karl Marx (1818–1920), a Prussian of Jewish descent, lived in London from 1849 until his death. He was one of the nineteenth century's pre-eminent philosophers; a close friend of Friedrich Engels and gave his name to the Marxist movement, founded on his philosophies. In 1867, Marx published the first volume of his seminal work, *Das Kapital*; most of which was reportedly written in the magnificent, round Reading Room of the old British Library. Charles Dickens also wrote a great many of his novels there and the two of them could often be found working in the library at the same time.

The Eastern Cemetery at Highgate also contains, amongst others, the graves of George Eliot, Leslie Stephen (father of Virginia Woolf and Vanessa Bell), George Henry Lewes, Henry Moore and the actor Sir Ralph Richardson. Sir Eyre Massey Shaw, first Head of the London Fire Brigade, is buried here too, and one of the most poignant of all the memorials is that dedicated to members of the London Fire Brigade who lost their lives while attempting to save others.

Mozart's Plaque
EBURY STREET, SW1

Wolfgang Amadeus Mozart was born in Salzburg, Austria, on 27 January 1756. His parents, Leopold, a violinist, and Anna Maria, had seven children, out of which only Wolfgang and his younger sister, Maria Anna, survived. By the age of four, Wolfgang was playing the harpsichord and, by the age of five, he was composing. Aged six he was playing before Vienna's Imperial Court. He was an instant favourite, particularly with the Empress, whose heart he stole after announcing he wanted to marry her daughter. With such a childhood, it seems inconceivable that Mozart was to die in ignominy and poverty and be buried in a communal pauper's grave at the age of 35.

Mozart and his family travelled to London in 1763. That year, aged seven, he made his London debut, accompanied by his four-year old sister. The concert was at Caldwell's Assembly Rooms, W1. In 1764–65, Mozart reputedly lived in two lodgings: at 180 Ebury Street, SW1, where he wrote his first symphony, and at 20 Frith Street, W1. Other noteworthy residents of Frith Street include John Logie Baird, the inventor of television.

In 1765, at the age of nine, Mozart gave a recital in the Hickford Rooms, Brewer Street. Shortly afterwards, he and his family left England.

The Golden Hinde
SAINT MARY OVERIE DOCK, SE1

The *Golden Hinde* (also called the *Golden Hind*) began life with the name the *Pelican*. She was sturdily constructed out of oak and built at Deptford, a shipyard set up for Henry VIII's navy. The oak used was grown in the area of Upper Norwood, now an area of South-East London – at this time the region was a heavily wooded part of the countryside.

In 1577, during the reign of Queen Elizabeth I, the great explorer Francis Drake set off in the *Golden Hinde*. He had already journeyed to the West Indies and his mission was now to circumnavigate the world and he did not return to England until 1580. After his epic voyage, Drake was knighted by Elizabeth at the Royal Naval Dockyard in Deptford. In 1588, the explorer was to gain further kudos, saving Elizabeth's empire from the Spanish Armada – famously insisting on finishing his game of bowls before setting off.

The *Golden Hinde* one sees today is a full-size reconstruction of the ship Sir Francis commanded; it is used as a working museum both for the entertainment of tourists and for the education of children. Children can spend a night camping on the boat learning about life as a sailor in the time of Sir Francis Drake.

ROYAL LONDON

London has been associated with royalty since before the beginning of written history. Explore the Tower of London, begun by William the Conqueror, and marvel at all the city's royal palaces, guarded by impressive soldiers.

Beefeater
TOWER HILL, EC3

The word 'Beefeater' is the affectionate nickname bestowed upon the 'Yeoman Warders of Her Majesty's Royal Palace and Fortress the Tower of London, and Members of the Queen's Body Guard of the Yeoman Guard Extraordinary'. Not surprisingly, the term 'Beefeater' is more widely known. There are 38 Yeoman Warders guarding the Tower, as well as the Chief Yeoman Warder and the Yeoman Gaoler. One warder is also appointed as guardian of the Tower's famous ravens.

The Tower of London is notorious for being haunted and many Beefeaters claim to have seen ghosts of those murdered here. One Warder claims to have been almost throttled by a pair of invisible hands while patrolling the Salt Tower one night. Dogs refuse to enter the Salt Tower, and to this day Warders are reluctant to go into it after dark.

The expression 'Beefeater' has unknown origins: some say it refers to the daily ration of meat Yeoman Warders were once given in return for their duties; other sources suggest it comes from the old English meaning of 'Eater' which is 'servant'; yet another theory is that the Yeoman Warders were expected to taste the food of royalty to ensure it was not poisoned.

Buckingham Palace
ST JAMES'S, SW1

Buckingham Palace is the Queen's official residence in London. Every year millions of tourists come here to watch the Changing of the Guard ceremony, to walk in nearby St James's Park and to try and catch a glimpse of the Queen herself. When the Queen is in residence her flag, the Royal Standard, is raised and can be seen flying on the Palace's roof.

In spite of Britain's extensive royal history, Buckingham Palace has only been the official home of the monarch since 1837. Until that time, Buckingham Palace was known simply as Buckingham House. It was built in 1633 by Lord Goring and was remodelled several times over the ensuing centuries. Its site was well chosen, standing as it does between two parks – St James's Park and Hyde Park – and at the end of a long tree-lined avenue, the Mall.

The house first became a royal residence when it was acquired by George III in 1761, but it was George IV who decided to convert it into a palace; he chose the architect John Nash to carry out his plans. Queen Victoria also added to the building. Today the Palace occasionally opens its doors to visitors. The interiors remain as sumptuous as they were during Victoria's reign, and the Palace houses a wealth of artworks and precious furniture.

Changing The Guard
BUCKINGHAM PALACE, SW1

The Changing of the Guard ceremony is one of London's most popular attractions; each day hundreds of people gather to watch it. It is a ceremony that is also performed at other royal residences, such as Windsor Castle in Berkshire.

It was not until 1837 that Buckingham Palace became the monarch's official residence in London, before then the official royal residence had been the Palace of Whitehall and, when that was almost destroyed by fire, the monarch moved to St James's Palace. The young Queen Victoria was the first monarch to live here properly; when she did so one officer and 44 men moved in to guard her.

At this time, the Changing of the Guard ceremony (when the old guard goes off duty and hands over the responsibility to the new guard) still took place at its former residence, St James's Palace, after which the renewed guard would move on to Buckingham Palace. It was not until 1963

that the ceremony began to take place at the Palace itself. The number of officers and men present changes between times when the Queen is in residence at the Palace and when she is elsewhere.

Fortnum & Mason
181 PICCADILLY, W1

The illustrious institution that is Fortnum & Mason started life as a Piccadilly market stall. In 1707, William Fortnum, a Royal footman, met Hugh Mason, a shop owner, and they went into business together. Subsequent generations of Fortnums and Masons kept the shop going; Fortnum's royal appointment was also continued by his descendants, this association helped to maintain constant royal patronage of the shop which continues today.

Fortnum & Mason has long been associated with luxury goods and remains the provider of delicacies from all over the world. The shop was one of the first to utilise overseas custom and it still receives regular orders from homesick expatriates all around the globe. Fortnums was also one of the earliest suppliers of 'ready meals', introducing tinned foods suitable for hiking trips and expeditions, and was the first shop in England to stock the products of a certain Mr Heinz.

The exquisite clock above the entrance door was unveiled in 1964. It was handmade by three of the country's leading clockmakers and depicts four-feet high figures of William Fortnum and Hugh Mason. The two men appear on the stroke of every hour.

Lambeth Palace
LAMBETH PALACE ROAD, SE1

Lambeth Palace was originally part of the Manor of Lambeth. In the twelfth century it was purchased by Archbishop Baldwin, and since then it has remained the official residence of the Archbishop of Canterbury.

The palace has seen a great deal of turbulent history: it was attacked by Wat Tyler and his followers in 1381; it was attacked twice in 1640 by poverty-stricken mobs and during the Civil War it was appropriated by Cromwell's troops and used as a prison. After Cromwell's victory, it became a place of entertainment where dances were held. Much sacrilegious vandalism took place during this time. When Charles II ascended the throne, Lambeth Palace was returned to the archbishop and repairs were undertaken.

The Tudor gatehouse (seen here) was built in 1485. It is a wonderful sight to behold when cruising along the River Thames, a perfectly preserved piece of London dating from before the Great Fire. This and the thirteenth-century crypt are the only original structures left intact; the rest of the building was restructured in the eighteenth and early nineteenth centuries.

Royal Observatory
GREENWICH, SE10

For many centuries, sailors struggled to find their way on rough seas, desperate for someone to discover the secret of determining longitude. It was widely accepted that the problem could be solved by careful study of astronomy and the science began to be more widely practised. In 1675, in recognition of this need, a young astronomer named John Flamsteed, was appointed the very first Astronomer Royal in the court of Charles II. On 10 August that same year the Royal Observatory on Greenwich Hill was begun.

The building was designed by Christopher Wren, the perfect choice as, not only was he the country's top architect, but he was also a keen astronomer. Flamsteed studied the stars from this spot for over 40 years; when he died he left behind his life's work, a vitally important study entitled *Historia Coelestis Britannica*. His successor was Edmund Halley, who discovered Halley's Comet and was the first person to map the stars of the southern hemisphere.

Today, visitors to the Observatory can see the original instruments used since the time of the first Astronomer Royals. Greenwich is positioned at longitude 0° and is recognised throughout the world in the horological expression GMT (Greenwich Mean Time).

Regent Street
W1

The sweeping architecture of Regent Street was designed by John Nash, one of England's most influential architects of the Regency period. Nash is most renowned for his Neo-Classical-style architecture, although he also designed buildings in the Gothic, Italian and Classical styles.

Regent Street was begun in 1811 and named after Nash's royal patron, George, Prince of Wales – the acting regent for his incapacitated father, King George III. The street connected Regent's Park (then known as Marylebone Park) to the Prince Regent's home, Carlton House. Nash's fine architecture originally included ornate colonnades but, sadly, these were demolished in 1848. The route was intended to be part-residential and part-commercial, accommodating expensive and fashionable shops. Today it is one of London's most popular shopping streets.

Nash also undertook other commissions for his royal patron, perhaps the most splendid, certainly the most unusual, of these was the Royal Pavilion at Brighton. Inspired by the architecture of India, Nash reconstructed the building into a phantasmagorical delight.

The Tower of London
TOWER HILL, EC3

There has been a tower on Tower Hill since very early times, definitely since the time of William the Conqueror and probably for many centuries before then. Archaeological evidence suggests that the site contained a fortress as far back as Roman times. The oldest part of the Tower that stands today dates back to the time of William I after he conquered England in 1066. This is known as the White Tower. In total, the Tower of London covers 18 acres with walls up to 90 ft high and 15 ft thick.

After William, many monarchs added to the Tower, most notably Henry III and Edward I. The Tower has been used for many and varied purposes: as a royal residence, an armoury, a treasury, a prison, a mint, a menagerie and a public-record house. The Tower also houses the city's oldest church, the Chapel of St John.

Several noble persons who were beheaded at the Tower are buried within its grounds, there is also a second graveyard – for the ravens. Legend decrees that if the ravens ever leave the Tower, the building and its country will fall. Today there are several resident ravens – whose wings are clipped just in case...

Houses of Parliament
WESTMINSTER BRIDGE, SW1

Although commonly known as the Houses of Parliament, this building's official title is the Palace of Westminster. A royal palace has stood on this site since the eleventh century; the first stone construction work took place in 1097 and the building was regularly added to in later centuries. The last monarch to live here was Henry VIII, who moved out after a fire in 1512. Since that time it has been a parliamentary building.

The site has witnessed a great many fires during its long history, but the worst, and most destructive, occurred in 1834. The fire was evocatively documented by J. M. W. Turner's painting, *Burning of the Houses of Parliament* (*c*. 1835). The building was utterly destroyed, with the exception of the oldest building: the stone walls of William Rufus's Great Hall survived.

Today, after 900 years, this is still in use, known as Westminster Hall.

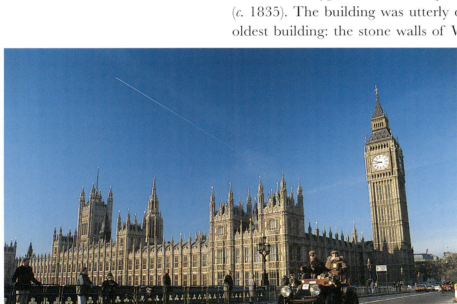

After the fire, a competition was held to find an architect to design the new Houses of Parliament. It was won by Charles Barry's Gothic-style plan. He began work in 1840 and the buildings were completed in 1870. The new Houses of Parliament include: St Stephen's Hall, Commons' Chamber, Lords' Chamber, Robing Room, Royal Gallery, Lords' Library, Commons' Library and dining rooms.

The King's Troop, RHA
WHITEHALL, SW1

The King's Troop, Royal Horse Artillery was formed in 1946 as The Riding Troop, Royal Horse Artillery. The Troop received its current name in 1947, after a visit by King George VI. When the King was asked to sign the visitors' book, he struck out the word 'Riding' and replaced it with 'King's'. That visitors' book remains in their barracks at St John's Wood, NW8. In memory of her father, Queen Elizabeth II decreed that the name remain unaltered during her reign.

The King's Troop is part of the Household Division and the only horsed artillery unit in the British Army. On state occasions, they fire a gun salute, which involves 41 guns if fired in a royal park, and 21 guns if fired elsewhere. State occasions include royal birthdays, visits from foreign Heads of State and the State Opening of Parliament. The regiment also fires the gun that signals the start and end of the two-minute silence on Remembrance Sunday. The King's Troop takes part in the annual Lord Mayor's Show and the Royal Tournament, where they perform their heart-stopping musical drive.

In 1997, the King's Troop provided the gun carriage for the funeral of Diana, Princess of Wales. The gun that was used bears a plaque recording the event.

Mounted Regiment of the Household Cavalry
WHITEHALL, SW1

The Household Cavalry makes up two of the seven regiments of the Household Division. Their two regiments, the Life Guards and the Blues and Royals, were amalgamated into the Household Cavalry in 1969. The Division's five other regiments are the Grenadier Guards, Coldstream Guards, Scots Guards, Irish Guards and Welsh Guards. Each regiment has the current sovereign as their Colonel-in-Chief. The Irish Guards were formed during the nineteenth century and the Welsh Guards were formed during the First World War, but the five other regiments have histories dating back to the seventeenth century.

The strength of the Household Cavalry is about 1,100. The Mounted Regiment is 300-strong, made up of both the Life Guards and the Blues and Royals. Their quarters are the Knightsbridge Barracks, SW7, which can house up to 303 soldiers and 273 horses.

The Mounted Regiment of the Household Cavalry can usually be seen guarding the Queen and her family at either London or Windsor. They also take part in the Queen's Birthday Parade, known as Trooping the Colour, which takes place each June.

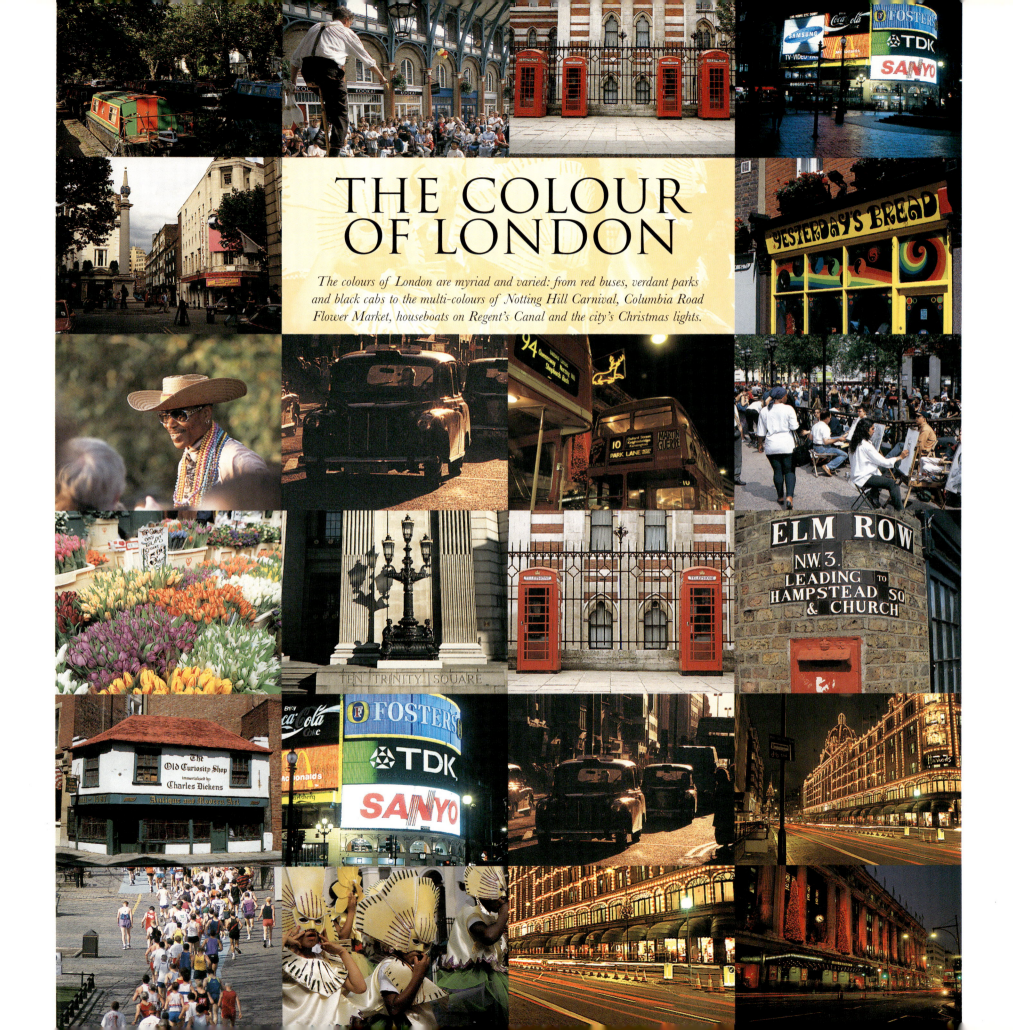

THE COLOUR OF LONDON

The colours of London are myriad and varied: from red buses, verdant parks and black cabs to the multi-colours of Notting Hill Carnival, Columbia Road Flower Market, houseboats on Regent's Canal and the city's Christmas lights.

London Taxis
OXFORD STREET, W1

A line of black cabs on Oxford Street is a familiar sight. Traditionally, London taxis were always black, but in recent years they have begun to appear in different colours. Drivers of these official taxis know their way around the city intimately – before they are granted a licence they have to take an exhaustive exam, known as 'the knowledge', in order to qualify. Acquiring 'the knowledge' can take up to three years.

The first taxis in London were called hackney carriages and were licensed from as early as the seventeenth century. These were single horse-drawn carriages, and originally only 300 licences were granted. In the nineteenth century, the hackney carriage gave way to the hackney cab, which could carry only two passengers. The next introduction was a 'growler', able to carry up to three passengers. Despite the introduction of motor vehicles, horse-drawn cabs could still be seen on the streets of London until as late as 1947.

Carnaby Street
W1

During the 1960s, the words 'Carnaby Street' became synonymous with youth and fashion. Anyone who was anyone was snapped shopping here, pop stars wrote songs about it, fashion magazines worshipped it, Harrods opened its own boutique in an attempt to lure their young clientele back; the name even became a recognised dictionary expression. Today, the street's shoppers are mostly tourists searching for the soul of swinging London as it was in the days of Jagger and Faithfull or McCartney and Asher; nevertheless, it is still an attractive street to walk through. It is small and pedestrianised, which makes it a pleasant road to wander along, and there are still plenty of shops and cafés to enjoy.

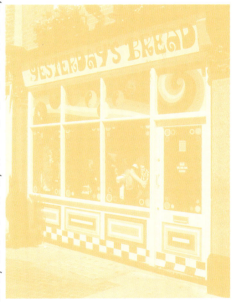

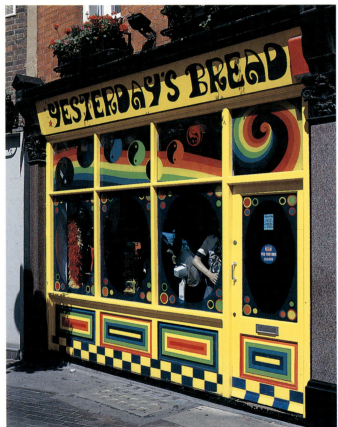

Just off Carnaby Street is Broadwick Street – the site of one of the most important medical discoveries ever made. It was in this street, in 1854, that Dr John Snow identified the cause of a local outbreak of cholera. He isolated the spread of the disease to the communal water pump in the street. In so doing, he realised that cholera could be passed on by water. His incredible scientific breakthrough has saved millions of lives throughout the world.

Notting Hill Carnival
W11

During the 1950s, racial tension in London had reached an horrendous peak, with black people often the victims of assault and ignorant crime. As a result many black-orientated social events were organised, where people knew they would be safe. West Indian musicians often played and their steel-band music became an evocative reminder of the traditions of Carnival. The black residents of Notting Hill soon began to hold regular steel-band dances that usually spilled out on to the streets.

The first actual carnival took place in Notting Hill on the August Bank Holiday weekend of 1966. It was a small procession, consisting of a few people in costumes and musicians playing steel drums. From this modest beginning, Notting Hill Carnival has grown to become one of Europe's largest arts festivals. The Carnival route runs along Ladbroke Grove, Westbourne Grove, Chepstow Road, Kensal Road and surrounding streets. It takes place on the last Sunday and Monday in August and is the most colourful and vibrant event on London's social calendar. The streets around Notting Hill are completely thronged with thousands of excited revellers, both participants in and spectators of the parade. The costumes are lavish and creative and the music and atmosphere hypnotically compelling.

Columbia Road Flower Market
COLUMBIA ROAD, E2

Columbia Road Flower Market began life as Columbia Market, a covered market financed by Baroness Burdett-Coutts in 1869. The baroness hoped her efforts would put an end to trading on the streets. The scheme was an expensive failure and, after a few years, the idea was more or less abandoned.

The flower market only takes place once a week, on Sunday mornings. It is a profusion of rich colour and wonderful scents and is one of the most perfect ways to begin a leisurely Sunday. The street market has remained at this site since the 1870s and now, as then, is still predominantly a cut flowers and plants market; although a few other shops and stalls sell food, drinks and crafts to market goers.

The origins of East End markets such as this one date back to the time when London's docks were at the height of their prosperity: perishable goods, such as flowers, were unloaded throughout the night and rushed to the nearest market to be sold as quickly as possible.

STREET PERFORMER
COVENT GARDEN, WC2

The street performers in Covent Garden are one of London's most famed attractions. Londoners and tourists alike come here to watch the many talented buskers who appear each day – all are licensed to ensure they are of a high standard.

The seventeenth-century architect Inigo Jones designed the Piazza and its magnificent St Paul's Church; which is the favoured outdoor area for street performers. Fittingly, St Paul's has become known as The Actors' Church due to the large number of artistes who were buried in the nearby churchyard. This arises from the proximity of Theatreland and the Royal Opera House. The church provides a suitably theatrical setting to the performers of today.

The tradition of street performers dates back through time immemorial. From the earliest recorded times, travelling players and minstrels have toured Britain appearing at festivities and feast days. These evolved into circuses and travelling-theatre companies who were eventually rivalled by the Punch and Judy Show. This spectacle (which originated in Italy) still takes place in Covent Garden today.

Double-Decker Buses
OXFORD STREET, W1

The big, red, double-decker bus is one of the city's most famous symbols, recognised the world over as a quintessential part of London. The first double-decker was called a 'Routemaster' and appeared for the first time in 1956. Before that time, Londoners found their way around the city on trolleybuses and, before trolleybuses were introduced, the city was dominated by trams and tramlines.

Two types of double-decker can be seen today: the old buses, which have open entrances at the back and a conductor to sell tickets, and the newer model with an access door at the front and, sadly, no conductor. For many, the first of these was immortalised in the 1960s film *Summer Holiday* in which Cliff Richard et al. drove a double-decker bus from London to Athens.

Sitting on the top deck of a double-decker is one of the best ways to see London as the height affords great views of the city. From the pavement or a car, the view is very limited, but from the top of a bus one can see the often spectacular architecture to full effect.

Houseboats on the Regent's Canal
LITTLE VENICE, W2

Oh, to be in England
Now that April's there.

'Home Thoughts from Abroad', *Robert Browning*

The Regent's Canal was begun in 1812 and took eight years to reach completion. It runs from an area near Paddington, in North London, to Limehouse in East London, where it joins the Thames. North of the city is the Grand Union Canal, which links the Regent's Canal to the waterways of Leicestershire and Northamptonshire. Until the advent of a comprehensive train system, this network of canals provided a vital route for goods transportation. Sadly for the boat masters, the railway proved to be both efficient and popular, and the canals' heyday was short-lived.

This area was named 'Little Venice' after comparisons made by the poets Robert Browning and Lord Byron (both of whom spent time living in Italy). It is an attractive, leafy part of the canal and one that has become a popular area for boating. Trips along the Regent's Canal are one of the best ways to see some of London's prettiest, and most well-hidden, sights. On a sunny day, there's no contest between the suggestion of a bus tour or a leisurely boat trip.

Road Sign
HAMPSTEAD, NW3

Hampstead is often referred to as 'the last village in London'. Somehow it manages to retain a small-community atmosphere while at the same time remaining an integral part of England's capital city. Some of the most exquisite examples of Georgian architecture in London can be found in Hampstead and many elegant roads and hidden-away streets provide fascinating, historical walks.

Centuries ago, Hampstead was already a noteworthy part of England, receiving a mention in the *Domesday Book*. It was an important tribal area in pre-Roman times and, as one of London's highest points, has retained its distinction ever since. It was here that a beacon was placed during the seventeenth-century war with Spain. If the beacon was lit, it alerted the whole of London to the fact that the Spanish Armada had landed.

In the sixteenth century a great flood was predicted that would drown all of London to purge the city of the vice it had fallen into. As the date, 1 February 1524, drew near, large crowds left their homes for Hampstead, hoping to be far enough out of London, and high enough above the city, to escape the flood waters. When the prediction was not fulfilled, the crowds went back down the hill and returned home.

HARRODS
KNIGHTSBRIDGE, SW1

The founder of Harrods, Charles Henry Harrod, started his career as an East End grocer and tea merchant in 1834. In 1861, his son, Charles Digby Harrod, took over his father's store and made many important changes to the type of goods stocked, concentrating on a higher luxury-goods content. In 13 years, Harrods' annual turnover increased from £1,040 to £52,000.

Harrods' motto, *Omnia Omnibus Ubique* ('all things for all people everywhere'), has led to many fantastic requests: from aeroplanes to alligators and baby elephants to grand pianos. At one time, Harrods built houses for their customers, sold yachts and even organised funerals. In 1885, the store opened personal credit accounts for the first time. Oscar Wilde was among the earliest to subscribe.

In 1898, Harrods installed Britain's first escalator. People flocked to see this fantastic spectacle. Mindful of the possibility of casualties, staff were instructed to be ready with emergency shots of brandy and smelling salts.

The store's instantly recognisable Brompton Road façade first appeared in 1901; it is constructed from terracotta. Every year, Harrods holds a sale in January and in July; with an average of 100,000 people attending every day. Many of these shoppers camp on the Brompton Road overnight hoping to be the first sale customer.

London Marathon
TOWER HILL, EC3

The London Marathon takes place each year on a Sunday in April or May. The marathon route encompasses 26 miles and 385 yards, from Greenwich to Westminster.

The first London Marathon was held in 1981, when approximately 6,000 runners took part. This number has expanded every year and the London Marathon is now the biggest in the world. Participants arrive from all over the world, ranging from the strictly amateur charity runners, often dressed in elaborate (and impeding) costumes, to the professionals competing for the prize money. There are always large numbers of disabled applicants, and the wheelchair race is one of the most skilful elements of the marathon, with competitors reaching breathtaking speeds.

The participants meet and line up on Greenwich's Blackheath, a place where public meetings and rallies have taken place throughout history: Wat Tyler and his followers gathered here in 1381; Henry V was met by huge crowds at the heath after winning at Agincourt and Charles II was welcomed back here, after the English Civil War.

In contrast to its healthy, sporting association, Blackheath received its name for an ominous reason: under the soil is a mass grave of those who died of the Black Death in the Middle Ages.

The Old Curiosity Shop
PORTSMOUTH STREET, WC2

The place ... was one of those receptacles for old and curious things...
There were suits of mail standing like ghosts in armour, here and there;
fantastic carvings brought from monkish cloisters; rusty weapons of various kinds;
distorted figures in china and wood, and iron, and ivory; tapestry,
and strange furniture that might have been designed in dreams.

The Old Curiosity Shop, *Charles Dickens, 1841*

This is believed to be the oldest shop in London and is, reputedly, the setting of Charles Dickens' novel *The Old Curiosity Shop*. The shop dates back to the sixteenth century and is now a listed building. It is one of the few buildings in London that gives a glimpse of how the city must have looked before the Great Fire of 1666.

The Old Curiosity Shop was one of Dickens' most popular works published in his lifetime. Many of his books first appeared in serial form and their direction was greatly affected by public reaction. This novel's heroine, Little Nell, provoked perhaps the largest amount of Dickens's public correspondence – letters urging him not to allow her to die. For once Dickens ignored the pleas of his public, believing her death essential to the plot's cause.

Selfridges
OXFORD STREET, W1

London's most famous department store was started by an American, H. Gordon Selfridge. The store opened on 15 March 1909 and on its first day received over 90,000 customers. By the end of its first week, Selfridges had welcomed its millionth customer.

In the 1920s, Selfridges opened the world's first television department and, in the 1930s, inspired by the flights of Louis Bleriot and Amy Johnson, it opened an aeroplane department!

When Selfridge retired in 1939, a member of his board, Andrew Holmes, took over. During the Second World War, the store was damaged several times, but remained open throughout. It was not until the 1970s that Selfridges' true war effort was revealed: in the basement was hidden the first-ever digital decoder, thereby allowing phone calls to be made from Number 10 Downing Street to the White House.

In the 1960s, Selfridges was bought by Charles Clore, a young salesman in the time of H. Gordon Selfridge. He added the Food Halls and oversaw the building of the prestigious Selfridge Hotel. Wonderful decorations had always graced the store during such celebrations as VE Day and Queen Elizabeth II's coronation, but during Clore's time the store also began its legendary Christmas displays. Every year hundreds of people queue up to view the first glimpse of Selfridge's Christmas windows.

Red Telephone Boxes
CROMWELL ROAD, SW7

The sight of red telephone boxes is quintessentially British. The first public telephone boxes to appear in Britain were erected in 1884. They were made of wood and glass and were considered unsightly: in later years, kiosks were inhospitably, and unaesthetically, constructed of concrete.

In 1924, as the demand for public telephones grew, the Post Office – which was then in charge of Britain's telephone system – decided to host a competition to find a new kiosk design. This was won by the now-legendary architect Giles Gilbert Scott (designer of Battersea Power Station). He designed two types of kiosk – one of which was employed in London and the other, a slightly less grand design, which was used elsewhere.

The telephone boxes pictured here are amongst the relatively few that still remain in England, as British Telecom continues to replace deteriorating kiosks with those of a modern design. However, Gilbert Scott's design has become an artistic classic and his kiosks can be found in art collections around the world. Visitors to Vienna are often taken aback to see an English telephone box outside Hundertwasser's House – the artist Friedrich Hundertwasser proclaimed it a miracle of modern design and took one home with him.

The Lights
PICCADILLY CIRCUS, W1

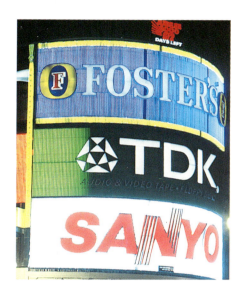

Piccadilly Circus is one of London's busiest areas. It is thronged with crowds throughout both day and night and visitors come from all over the world to see its famous lights. The earliest of these illuminations were seen in 1910 – to the abject horror of the Circus's residents. Amongst the first companies to advertise here were Bovril and Schweppes. The tradition has continued ever since, and today household names such as Coca Cola and Samsung pay some of the world's largest advertising fees to see their names in lights.

Piccadilly Circus was built in 1819. Originally the network of surrounding roads met here at a crossroads, but within a few years it had developed into an elegant circle ('circus') of buildings and became an address of great distinction.

The area around Piccadilly has long been associated with the royal area of St James's, the two regions became famous in the eighteenth century for the many Gentlemen's Clubs that lined the streets – names including Brooks', White's and Almack's. Regency dandies spent inordinate amounts of time, and money, at the clubs and the very word 'Piccadilly' evolved from 'picadill' – a neck ruff worn by fashionable men.

Portrait Artists
LEICESTER SQUARE, WC2

Amateur portrait painters can often be found around Piccadilly and Leicester Square. The square is a haven for tourists, and because it is pedestrianised is a great place for artists to set up without being disturbed. Many artists stay until late in the evening, sketching their customers by the bright lights emanating from the cinemas, clubs, cafés and restaurants around them.

In the eighteenth century, Leicester Square was a beautifully laid out and exceedingly well-appointed garden; the crowning glory of Leicester House, one of London's most prestigious addresses. In time, houses began to be built around the edge of the square – one of the early tenants was the famous writer and engraver William Hogarth, and Joshua Reynolds, founder of the Royal Academy, also lived here.

As the nineteenth century took hold, central London became more

and more built up and the residents of Leicester Square started to move out; making way for the shops and businesses that sprang up – among these was a renowned Turkish bathhouse. Today, the square is one of the capital's most crowded places to be on a Friday or Saturday night.

Old Gas Lights
TRINITY SQUARE, EC3

... when I am stronger and can choose what I'm to do,
O Leerie, I'll go round at night and light the lamps with you!

For we are very lucky with a lamp before the door,
And Leerie stops to light it as he lights so many more.

'The Lamplighter', *Robert Louis Stevenson*

 These lights, now fitted with electricity, began life as gas lamps. Electric street lighting was first attempted in 1858, but it was distrusted and did not gain popularity until the beginning of the twentieth century.

Before the nineteenth century, the streets of London were dimly lit by oil lamps, candlelight from nearby houses and the light of the moon and stars. On a cloudy night, or in sparsely populated areas, the roads were terrifying. Highwaymen and thieves thrived and crime rates were exorbitant.

In 1807, to celebrate the birthday of the flamboyant Prince Regent (later George IV), Pall Mall was illuminated by gas light before an astounded audience of well-wishers. This was the first time that gas had been seen in London.

Gas lighting provided a welcome respite from the treacherous darkness and London went from being the darkest capital in Europe to become one of the brightest.

Seven Dials
WC2

The peculiar character of these streets, and the close resemblance each one bears to its neighbour, by no means tends to decrease the bewilderment in which the unexperienced wayfarer through 'the Dials' finds himself involved.

Sketches by Boz, *Charles Dickens, 1836*

Seven Dials stands not far from Neal's Yard. It links Mercer Street, Monmouth Street, Earlham Street and Shorts Gardens, and connects Covent Garden with Soho. Originally, as its name suggests, it was the central point of seven streets: Little St Andrew's Street, Great St Andrew's Street, Great Earl Street, Little Earl Street, Little White Lion Street, Great White Lion Street and Queen Street. During the eighteenth and nineteenth centuries, it was a renowned meeting place of criminals, and somewhere to be avoided at all costs after dark. Today, the surrounding streets contain unique shops, cafés and the Cambridge Theatre.

The column which can be seen at the centre of Seven Dials is a copy of the original, which was pulled down in the eighteenth century. The top of the pillar sports six sundials – the seventh is created by the central spike at the column's top.

Speakers' Corner
HYDE PARK, W2

Hyde Park covers an area of 340 acres. It first became a royal park in 1536, when Henry VIII seized it from its original landowners in order to use it as a hunting ground. Here, he chased the indigenous wild boar, deer and wild bulls.

In the seventeenth century it was opened to the public and, in 1872, a new law led to the concept of Speakers' Corner. This law legalised all public speaking with only three constraints to be taken into consideration:

1. the speech must not be deemed obscene;
2. the speech must not be deemed blasphemous; and
3. the speech must not incite riotous acts or any other breach of the peace.

Anyone who so desired was therefore able to declaim on the subject of their choice quite freely and the tradition continues today. Sunday visitors to Hyde Park are still assured of seeing an orator expounding on his or her beliefs. Speakers' Corner is renowned for its eccentricity and remains one of London's most individual and enduring traditions, as well as a lively demonstration of truly free speech.

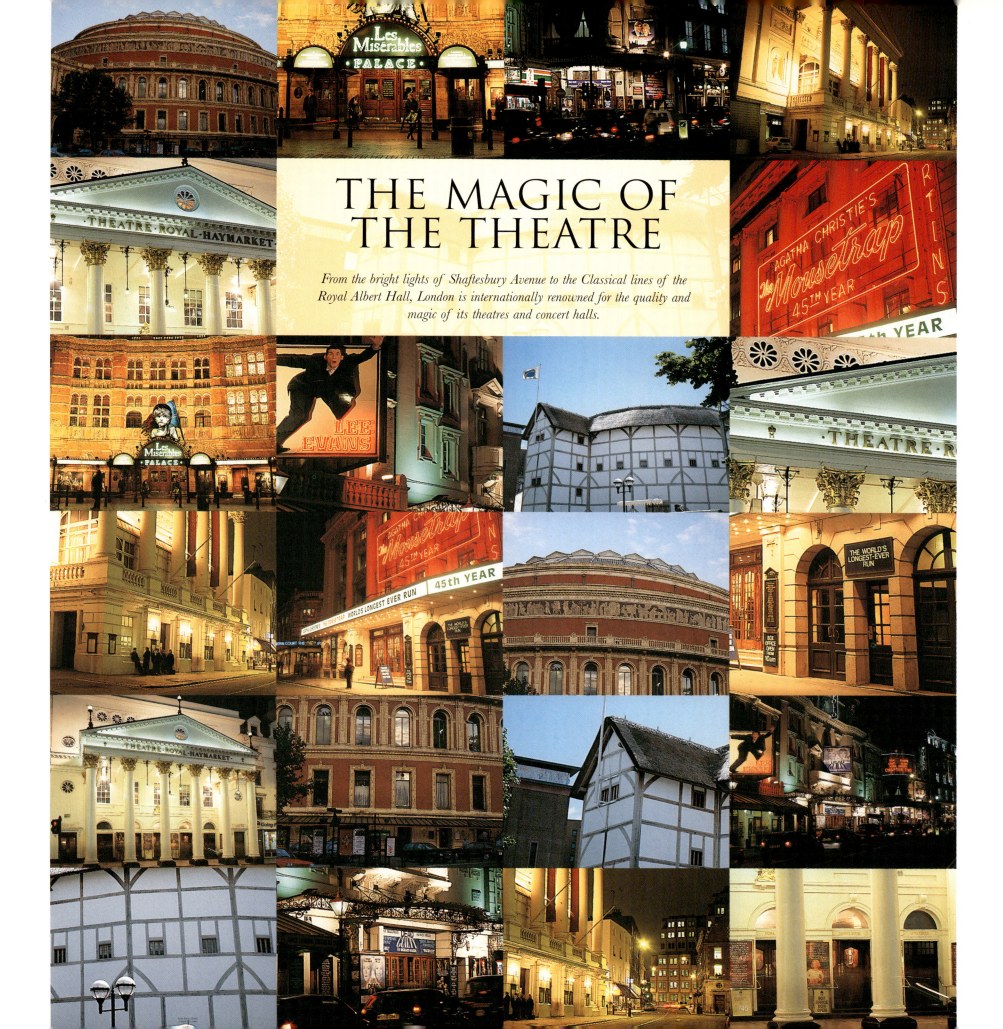

THE MAGIC OF THE THEATRE

From the bright lights of Shaftesbury Avenue to the Classical lines of the Royal Albert Hall, London is internationally renowned for the quality and magic of its theatres and concert halls.

Royal Albert Hall
KENSINGTON GORE, SW7

In 1852, the Kensington-Gore Estate was purchased for the public; using funds from profits made in the Great Exhibition of 1851. It was Prince Albert who first suggested building a hall here, it was to be called the Central Hall of Arts and Sciences. After his death in 1861, however, Queen Victoria chose to name the hall after her much-mourned husband. She laid the foundation stone in 1867 and declared the Albert Hall open in 1872.

Since its grand opening ceremony, the hall has been host to a variety of events, including the Titanic Band Memorial Concert in 1912 and Yehudi Menuhin's first appearance, aged 13. Today the hall is renowned for its annual Festival of Remembrance and the Proms, as well as hosting pop concerts (the Beatles, Rolling Stones and Jimi Hendrix all played here in the Sixties), ballets, sporting events, lectures, film premieres, opera and the British Fashion Awards.

The Royal Albert Hall also has a ghostly history. Several members of staff report seeing a couple of young women walking along and talking animatedly. The reports claim that they look real – until they disappear through one of the walls. Other apparitions include the ghost of the organ builder, Father Willis, and a strange man dressed in white, who has been glimpsed wandering across the stage during performances.

Shakespeare's Globe
BANKSIDE, SE1

In 1599, the Globe Playhouse was built roughly 200 yards from where the present Globe Theatre stands today. The Playhouse saw regular performances of William Shakespeare's plays before it burned down in 1613. A second Playhouse was instantly built on the same site. When Shakespeare died in 1616, his plays continued to be performed at the theatre.

In 1642, the Globe Playhouse was closed by the Puritans who disapproved of the sentiments evinced in the Bard's works and the hilarity they provoked. Two years later, they destroyed the building to the extent that even the foundations were buried without trace.

In 1971, Sam Wanamaker attempted to find the remains of Shakespeare's theatre. Finding no trace of it, he set up a scheme to rebuild the Globe. Sadly he died in 1993, four years before the theatre was officially opened. The theatre's architect, Theo Crosby, also died in 1994. However, their work has become a remarkable monument both to them and to Shakespeare. The main theatre (with capacity for an audience of 1,401) hosts plays and entertainment for five months of the year and serves as an education centre for the remaining seven months. There is also the Inigo Jones Theatre, which is being built to the sixteenth-century architect's original designs for an unknown theatre. It will seat 330 people. The plans for this theatre were discovered recently in Cambridge.

Theatre Royal
HAYMARKET, SW1

The Haymarket's Theatre Royal is one of the most elegant theatres in London and has housed some of the world's best-loved plays and operettas. The famous actors and writers associated with the theatre are legion.

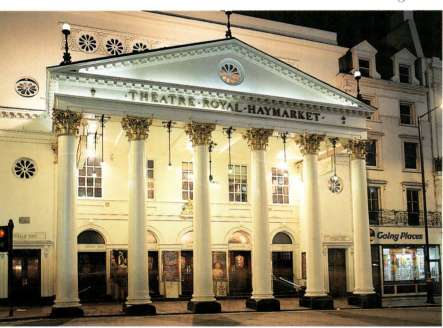

The first theatre built in the Haymarket was a few streets away from the site of the present-day theatre. It was known as the Little Theatre and was built by a carpenter named John Potter. It opened on 29 December 1720. The theatre remained on this site for exactly 100 years – until it was pulled down in 1820.

Today's theatre retains its 'Royal' title from a licence granted to the Little Theatre in 1758. The theatre became very popular with royalty and the aristocracy, particularly during the years 1793–94 when the Drury Lane Theatre was under reconstruction. On 3 February 1794 King George III visited the Little Theatre – in the desire to see their monarch, 20 people were killed in the crush.

In 1821, the theatre seen today was opened. Its first performance was Sheridan's *The Rivals*, a play that is still performed regularly. In 1837, the famous author and actor Benjamin Webster became the theatre's new manager. His time there was most noteworthy because he became the first-ever manager to take his company on tour.

Royal Opera House
COVENT GARDEN, WC2

In 1732, the first theatre was built on this site, housing plays, operas, concerts and the occasional ballet. During the mid-1700s, George Friedrich Handel composed a great many operas for the theatre and it began to gain a worthy reputation. Sadly, in 1808, many of Handel's original manuscripts, along with his organ, perished when the building caught fire.

A year later, a replacement theatre, built to a Classical Greek design, was opened. It saw a profusion of premieres and important performances – Mozart, Verdi, Mrs Siddons, Edmund Kean, William Charles Macready and John Kemble are just a few of the names associated with it. Sadly this second theatre stood for only 47 years until it, too, was burned down in 1856.

In 1858, the third Opera House (seen here) was opened; by this time it had become recognised as pivotal in the world of opera and ballet and the words 'Covent Garden' had become internationally synonymous with culture and opulence. The world's greatest names have appeared on its stage – Patti, Callas, Domingo, Carreras, Pavarotti, Nureyev and Fonteyn to name just a handful.

Today the Royal Opera House is undergoing extensive refurbishment, but promises to be as magnificent as ever when it reopens.

Palace Theatre

CAMBRIDGE CIRCUS, W1

In London the noblest surviving building –
in my opinion more impressive within and without than Covent Garden –
is the Royal English Opera House ... now called the Palace Theatre.

'The Palace Theatre', *John Betjeman*

On 15 December 1888, the first stone was laid for a new building, designed by the architects Thomas Calcutt and C. H. Holloway for the celebrated theatrical personality Richard D'Oyly Carte. The entrepreneur was a fervent supporter of Gilbert and Sullivan and wished to build a house for English Opera. The Royal English Opera House opened in January 1891. Sadly, the lack of English operas forced D'Oyly Carte to sell his new building to the Drury Lane theatre owner Sir Augustus Harris. After a few alterations, it was reopened as the Palace Theatre on 10 December 1892.

For many years the theatre was a music hall; in 1914 it became a revue hall and it has also hosted ballets, operettas, musicals and, with the growth of Hollywood, films. The first film shown here was in 1921; it was *Pollyanna*.

From 1972-80, the Palace Theatre hosted Andrew Lloyd Webber's international hit musical *Jesus Christ Superstar*. Since 1985 it has been home to the astoundingly successful Cameron Mackintosh production *Les Misérables*.

Theatreland by Night
SHAFTESBURY AVENUE, WC2

Shaftesbury Avenue was named after the 7th Earl of Shaftesbury – to whose memory the statue of Eros was also dedicated. The Earl had dedicated his life to helping the poor around this area, which was once one of the worst slums in London.

The street was opened in 1886 and runs between Piccadilly Circus and New Oxford Street. It has become synonymous with London's theatres, a reputation it acquired almost instantly – within the first 20 years, six theatres had opened along the road.

Shaftesbury Avenue runs through Soho, one of the most densely built-up and lively places in London. Formerly known as the red-light district, it has recently been transformed into a gourmet's haven, with streets replete with trendy bars and cafes and exotic restaurants. There is still plenty of sleaze alongside the glitz, however, taking the area light years away from when it was land owned jointly by the Church and a leper colony. The lands were later appropriated by Henry VIII for hunting – the region takes its name from the hunting cry 'So-Ho'.

St Martin's Theatre
WC2

St Martin's Theatre was built in 1916, in the middle of the First World War. It seats 550 customers and has staged a great many plays by important playwrights, including John Galsworthy and Clemence Dane; however, it has become most famous for its world-record-breaking run of Agatha Christie's *The Mousetrap*. The play began showing here in 1974, two years before the death of the author.

Agatha Christie (1890-1976) began writing detective fiction in 1918. Her first novel was *The Mysterious Affair At Styles*, in which she introduced the Belgian detective Hercule Poirot. In all she wrote 76 detective novels, which have been translated into many languages. These still sell in immense numbers throughout the world. In 1971, Agatha Christie was created a Dame of the British Empire.

The name of Agatha Christie is renowned, and revered, internationally. It is this extraordinary fame that has assisted with the popularity of *The Mousetrap*'s theatrical career. As well as theatre-going Londoners, tourists from all over the world flock to see the world's longest-running play by the crime world's most famous creator.

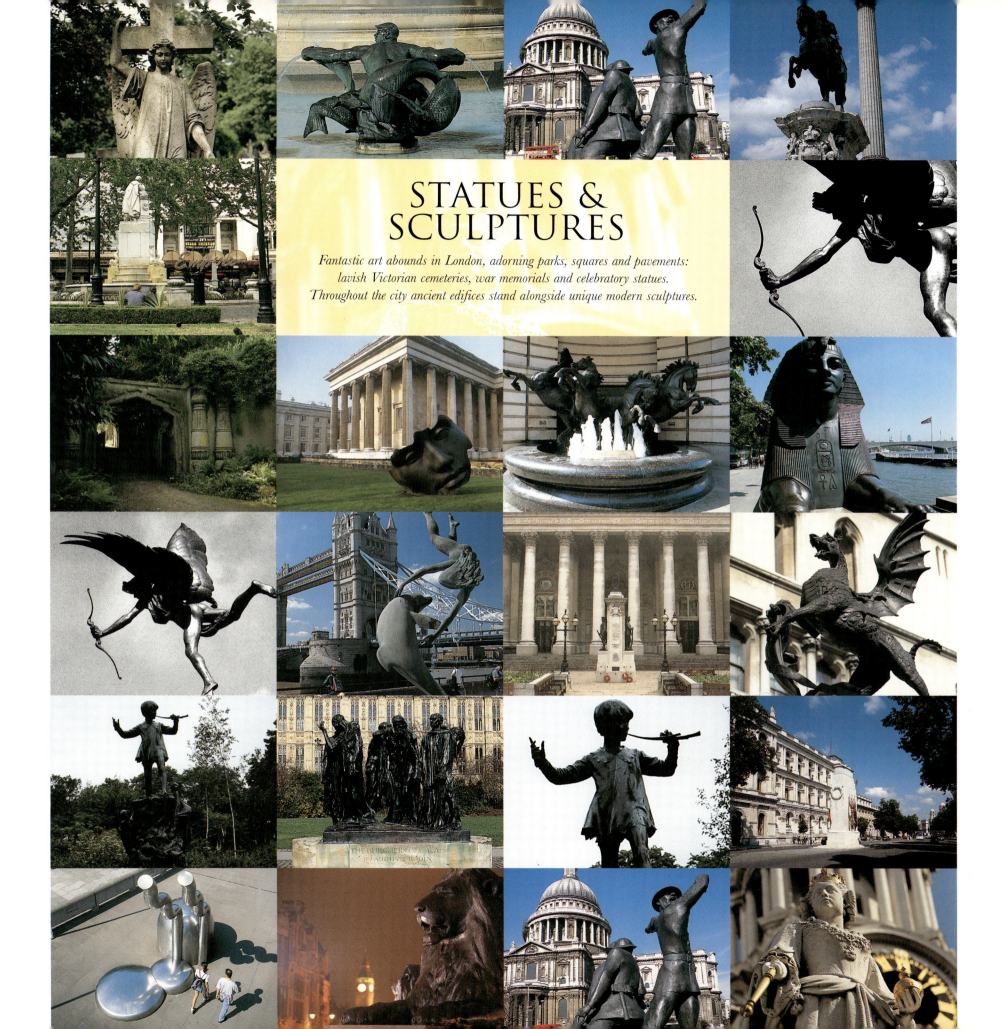

STATUES & SCULPTURES

*Fantastic art abounds in London, adorning parks, squares and pavements:
lavish Victorian cemeteries, war memorials and celebratory statues.
Throughout the city ancient edifices stand alongside unique modern sculptures.*

Gravestone
HIGHGATE CEMETERY, N6

Highgate Cemetery lies in two parts: the Eastern Cemetery and the Western Cemetery; between them they encompass 17½ acres. The cemetery was opened in 1839; at the time, this area was still several miles outside London. The land was laid out as a formal park and became a popular place for city dwellers to visit on days out.

Highgate has many fantastic and elaborate tombs. The architecture changes visibly with each Victorian fad – from Egyptian to Gothic to Neo-Classical – within a few metres of land. Alongside the tombs of the famous are many less well-known tombs whose inscriptions bear witness to poignant and tragic circumstances, such as parents whose children all died in infancy or the cautionary tale of 17-year-old Emma Cray who was killed in 1849 after her dress caught fire. However, there are also moments of humour which leave a marked impression of the personality of the deceased, such as the wonderful

Gordon Bell
(Middle name Ernest, though he placed no importance on it)
20.12.1942–17.3.1995
'Tomorrow do thy worst for I have lived today.'

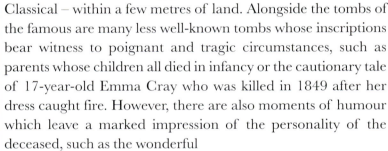

Dramatic Mask

BRITISH MUSEUM, WC1

This is London's oldest museum. Its initial collection of treasures came from the arts collection of Sir Hans Sloane; an idea suggested by Sloane in his will. Over the following years, the government acquired more exhibits and the museum was opened to the public in 1759.

At first the rules of entry were ridiculously prohibitive: a written application had to be made; if approved, a ticket would be issued – but only 10 people per hour were allowed tickets and the museum was only open for three hours a day. Visitors were accompanied by a porter at all times and women were not allowed in without a male escort! Unrestricted access was finally granted in 1879.

The museum is home to an awe-inspiring array of antiquities and curiosities. The most famous of these include the Elgin Marbles (taken from the Parthenon in Athens); Egyptian mummies; the seventh-century Sutton Hoo treasure; the Lindisfarne Gospels (also from the seventh century) and the Mildenhall Treasure. The latter dates from the fourth century and was discovered in 1942, by a Suffolk farmer ploughing his field.

This mask sculpture was created by Igor Mitoraj. It alternates between being displayed here and being shown elsewhere in Britain and Europe.

Cenotaph
WHITEHALL, SW1

The Cenotaph is one of the most poignant landmarks in London. Always kept scrupulously clean and tidy, it is the central monument to all those who died in the two World Wars. Each year on Remembrance Sunday (the Sunday closest to 11 November), the Queen and the Royal Family make a pilgrimage here to listen to the Service of Remembrance and to lay a commemorative wreath. It is a truly solemn moment. For one moment in the year, there is absolute silence on what is normally one of the busiest roads in the city. The service is televised throughout Britain in honour of all those who fought to keep their country safe.

The Cenotaph is an austere, stone, block-like monument, decorated simply. Two of the sides and the top of the monument bear carved, be-ribboned wreaths above which are the dates of the First World War in roman numerals; the other two sides each carry three flags, including the Union Jack and ensigns of the Army, Royal Air Force and Royal Navy, on gold-painted flagpoles, above which are the dates of the Second World War, also in roman numerals.

EROS

PICCADILLY CIRCUS, W1

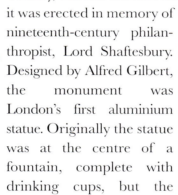

The statue of Eros, at Piccadilly Circus, has become an unofficial symbol of London. The steps at the base of the statue have become a popular meeting place and are usually crowded with people.

The statue actually represents an Angel of Christian Charity, but has become known as Eros, the god of Love; it was erected in memory of nineteenth-century philanthropist, Lord Shaftesbury. Designed by Alfred Gilbert, the monument was London's first aluminium statue. Originally the statue was at the centre of a fountain, complete with drinking cups, but the water is no longer turned on. All around the underside of the basin is the following inscription:

Erected by public subscription to Antony Ashley Cooper KC, seventh Earl of Shaftesbury, born April XXVIII MDCCCI, died October I MDCCCLXXXV. During a public life of half a century he developed the influence of his station, the strong sympathies of his heart and the great powers of his mind. To honouring God by serving his fellow men, an example of his order, a blessing to this people and a name to be by them ever gratefully remembered.

Fountain Statue
TRAFALGAR SQUARE, WC2

The fountain is the centrepiece of Trafalgar Square and one of London's best-loved landmarks. This bronze statue is sited opposite a female counterpart, both statues spew forth water as does the spout in the centre. During the 1970s, the fountain became a significant part of the New Year's festivites as drunken revellers climbed into the base and danced naked; this was soon brought to an end and the fountain is now strongly guarded on New Year's Eve. The square however remains London's most popular place to be on the stroke of midnight each New Year. Big Ben can be seen from Trafalgar Square and thousands of people gather here each 31 December to listen to the famous chimes.

The square stands on the site of the former royal stables, dating back to the time of King Edward I (1272–1307), but was laid out in its current form in 1840. The architect of this plan was Sir Charles Barry, who also designed the Houses of Parliament.

LEICESTER SQUARE
WC2

In the centre of Leicester Square is an enclosed area of gardens. The enclosure was a gift to the people of London from the nineteenth-century MP Albert Grant. Over 100 years later, the area was given a face lift and reopened, by the Queen, in 1992. In the centre stands a fountain and around the edge of the paved area surrounding it are bronze plaques naming each country of the Commonwealth, their capital and their distance from London in both kilometres and miles.

The fountain is topped by a statue of England's greatest playwright, William Shakespeare. In front of it is a bronze of Charlie Chaplin (the base of his statue reads: *The Comic Genius Who Gave Pleasure To So Many*) and in all four corners of the gardens stand a bust, each one of a famous resident of the area. The busts represent the painter Joshua Reynolds, the scientist Isaac Newton, the pioneer anatomist John Hunter and the illustrator William Hogarth.

Lion
TRAFALGAR SQUARE, WC2

There are four bronze lions in Trafalgar Square, which lie protectively at the base of Nelson's Column, each measuring 20 ft in length and 22 ft in height. They were designed by the great artist Sir Edwin Landseer, and were laden with mourning wreaths after his death. The lions have become one of London's best-loved features. They are wonderfully tactile and every day, hundreds of tourists are photographed clambering, trying to get as close as they possibly can to a paw, at least!

Trafalgar Square is also home to several other statues: King George IV on horseback; General Charles James Napier, a memorial erected by public subscription; and Major General Sir Henry Havelock, dedicated to the memory of him and all his troops.

Behind the open-mouthed lion, pictured here, can be seen the lighted face of Big Ben. In the times when the Palace of Westminster was the home of the monarch and Trafalgar Square was the Royal Mews, Whitehall, the street leading from Trafalgar Square to Westminster, was a well-trodden route.

Nelson's Column
TRAFALGAR SQUARE, WC2

Charles Barry's nineteenth-century designs for Trafalgar Square were to commemorate Admiral Horatio Viscount Nelson's victory at the Battle of Trafalgar in 1805. Tragically, it was at this battle that Nelson received the wound that was to prove fatal. The column stands 145 ft high and was built by public subscription. The statue of Nelson was designed by E. H. Baily. The base contains four bronze reliefs depicting his four great naval victories: Cape St Vincent (1797), The Nile (1798), Copenhagen (1801) and Trafalgar (1805); the bronze came from cannons captured during Nelson's campaigns.

Looking to the south of the column, one can see a bronze statue of Charles I on horseback. After Charles I (1600-49) was executed during the English Civil War (1649-60), Oliver Cromwell ordered this statue to be destroyed. However it was saved by Royalists who hid it for the duration of the war. In 1675, during the reign of Charles II, the statue was re-erected. Charles I was executed on 30 January 1649 and each year, on the anniversary of his death, members of the Royal Stuart Society visit the statue to lay a commemorative wreath.

Peter Pan Statue
KENSINGTON GARDENS, W8

J. M. Barrie's famous story of *Peter Pan* was first written as a play; since then it has become one of the best-known children's books of all time. This magical statue has stood in Kensington Gardens since 1912. It is sculpted in bronze and was designed by George Frampton. Peter is depicted playing his pipes (Barrie's Classical allusion to the pagan god Pan) to the profusion of fairies and animals that play around the statue's base.

Peter Pan was first performed in 1904 and quickly enraptured audiences everywhere. So absorbing was the story of the little boy who never grew up, that it continued to be performed year after year and is still a popular Christmas pantomime. The play was also the first to feature mechanical wires that assisted the characters to 'fly'. In 1906, Barrie wrote the story *Peter Pan in Kensington Gardens*, which is why this statue stands on this site.

Even more important than its role in providing millions of children with the pleasure of a wonderful story, *Peter Pan* has also helped a great many very ill children. All royalties earned by Barrie's creation are now given to the Great Ormond Street Children's Hospital in WC1.

Queen Anne's Statue
ST PAULS' CATHEDRAL, EC4

This statue that stands in front of St Paul's Cathedral was erected in memory of Queen Anne (1665–1714), during whose reign the cathedral was built. The statue was made by Richard Belt and unveiled in 1885 – it is a replacement for the original, made by Francis Bird, which had decayed into an almost irreparable state. The original was rescued by the Victorian travel writer Augustus Hare, who took it to his private house in Sussex.

The second statue purportedly copies the original. Anne's regal status is emphasised by her golden crown and the golden orb and sceptre she carries in her hands. At the base of her statue are representative figures of England, Ireland, North America and France.

Queen Anne was a popular monarch who ruled for 12 years. She was married to the son of the King of Denmark. Sadly, although Anne gave birth to 18 children, only one of these survived infancy and he died at the age of 11. Due to the lack of an heir, the throne of England passed to the Hanoverian line; the first of these was George I, a king who spoke only a few words of English at his coronation.

Sculpture
SOUTH BANK, SE1

This intriguing sculpture is by William Pye, and is entitled *Zemran*. It was unveiled in 1972, after it was presented it to the Greater London Council. Not far away stands another important sculpture, a bronze bust of Nelson Mandela, the influential freedom fighter and the first black president of South Africa. The area in which these statues stand is a haven for buskers and street artists; second-hand book fairs are also held here regularly. It is a great area to sit with friends or alone, to eat and drink and enjoy the atmosphere.

Walking away from the South Bank, one can either head east into the City of London, north to the Strand, Trafalgar Square and Covent Garden, south to Vauxhall or west to Westminster. The path along the river towards the Houses of Parliament takes the walker alongside the newly built London Aquarium.

The South Bank area was originally marshland, until it was drained and landscaped to allow a private house to be built here in the early eighteenth century. The house's owner was Charles Bascom. He called his house Belvedere and opened the gardens to the public. Today all that remains of his enterprise is a road named Belvedere that runs behind the Royal Festival Hall.

Egyptian Sphinx
VICTORIA EMBANKMENT, WC2

This is one of two bronze sphinxes cast to stand guard at the base of Cleopatra's Needle, which was unveiled in 1878. The sphinx is a mythical beast with the body of a lion and the face of a human; it is also supposed to have magical powers, including the gift of prophecy. These sphinxes wear the headdresses of Egyptian pharaohs, including the royal symbol of a serpent. The serpent was a symbol of protection, said to spit poison at enemies of the pharaoh.

When Cleopatra's Needle arrived in England it heightened an already popular fad – a slavish preoccupation with all things Egyptian. The fashionable world bought Egyptian-influenced art, decorated rooms in Egyptian style and even built their tombs to look like Egyptian architecture.

On 4 April 1917, the sphinxes and Cleopatra's Needle received a rude shock when savage shrapnel from a German bomb blasted them – both sphinxes and the obelisk's base still bear the scars. Fittingly, across the road stands a bronze statue of a woman and two children, inscribed with the words: *To the British nation from the grateful people of Belgium 1914-1918.*

171

Egyptian Avenue
WESTERN CEMETERY, HIGHGATE, N6

This magnificent stone gateway heralds the start of Egyptian Avenue; at one time the most expensive and prestigious place in which to purchase one's family tomb. The avenue leads to the Lebanon Circle – so-called because of the ancient Cedar of Lebanon which stands in the centre of the circus of tombs. Cedars of Lebanon were the trees reputedly used in the building of the Hanging Gardens of Babylon; this particular tree is believed to date back to the seventeenth century.

The Western Cemetery at Highgate is home to a great many elaborate tombs, although it also contains many comparatively understated, simple monuments. Among the many thousands of people who have been entombed here are the poet Christina Rossetti, her sister-in-law Elizabeth Siddal (wife of Dante Rossetti), the controversial female author Radclyffe Hall, circus owner George Wombwell, Charles Cruft

(founder of the Crufts dog show), the Dickens family tomb (minus Charles, who was buried at Westminster Abbey), the scientist and inventor Michael Faraday, the painter Edwin Landseer, the cricketer Frederick Lilleywhite, the actor Samuel Phelps, Frederick Tennyson (brother of the more famous Alfred) and Robert Addis – whose claim to fame is the invention of the toothbrush.

Firemen's War Memorial
ST PAUL'S CATHEDRAL, EC4

The bronze Firemen's War Memorial was designed by John W. Mills; it was unveiled in 1991 – 130 years after the founding of the London Fire Brigade.

Although earlier attempts had been made at fire-fighting, the London Fire Brigade did not come into existence until 1861. Its first chief was Sir Eyre Massey who trained his recruits to a highly efficient level and remained at the helm for 30 years. He died in 1908, at the age of 80, and is buried in the Eastern Cemetery at Highgate.

William the Conqueror was the first ruler to attempt to instil an awareness of the dangers of fire in his people, but his rigid laws about the dousing of fires and candles at night were slowly forgotten, or ignored, through the ensuing centuries. In the early seventeenth century, fire-fighting equipment was in existence – however, it proved fairly useless at fighting minor fires and utterly ineffective during the Great Fire of London.

In 1696, Joseph Hay, owner of Hay's Wharf, set up a fire-fighting scheme with two neighbouring wharf owners. They employed six firemen. Ironically, the wharves were decimated in the Great Fire of Tooley Street in 1861 – the fire that finally led to the founding of the London Fire Brigade.

War Memorial
ROYAL EXCHANGE, EC3

The Royal Exchange has played an important part in London life in many areas other than trade. This poignant memorial to those who died in the First and Second World Wars stands in front William Tite's magnificent building and every year, on Remembrance Sunday, a service is held here. Wreaths of poppies are placed at the base of the memorial, a tradition dating back to the end of the First World War. Poppies are symbolic of all those cut down in action; the first were used in memory of those killed in the fields of Flanders and the Somme – which once were glorious poppy fields before the fighting transformed them into mudlocked, trench-scarred graveyards.

During the Second World War, a bomb hit the ground in front of the Exchange creating the biggest crater seen in London throughout the Blitz: it measured 1,800 sq ft. Eighty people were killed. The Royal Engineers constructed a temporary bridge over the crater to keep the traffic flowing in spite of the war.

In a less sombre mood, in the mid-nineteenth century the Royal Exchange witnessed the opening of Britain's first public loos – for men only – and in 1936, Edward VIII's accession to the throne was announced on the steps of the Royal Exchange.

The Burghers of Calais
HOUSES OF PARLIAMENT, SW1

This distinguished bronze stands in front of the Houses of Parliament, in the Victoria Tower Gardens. It is a replica of a bronze created by the French sculptor, Auguste Rodin, for the town of Calais in 1895. Rodin was renowned for the copies he made of his own works and he unveiled this statue himself in 1913, just four years before his death.

The original statue was erected as a monument to the fourteenth-century heroes of Calais who were willing to die in order to save their city from destruction. In 1340, the town's burghers surrendered themselves to the marauding Edward III, wearing halters round their necks as a symbol of their oppression. Their selfless actions saved their beloved town and its people.

Rodin was born in Paris in 1840. He is perhaps the greatest sculptor that ever lived, prolific in output and exquisite in detail. His works are internationally recognisable and include *The Thinker* (1880), *The Kiss* (1886), *The Eternal Idol* (1889), *The Hand of God* (1898) and *The Gates of Hell* (1880-1917).

GRIFFIN
TEMPLE BAR, EC4

A griffin, sometimes called a 'gryphon', is a mythical creature and the unofficial symbol of the City of London. The first recorded mention of a griffin dates back to the fourteenth century. Reputedly it is a winged beast with the body, hind legs and tail of a lion and the head, wings and chest of an eagle. This bronze, which tops Horace Jones's memorial to Nelson, was designed by Charles Birch.

Temple Bar is on Fleet Street and the Strand, on the site that was once the marker of the western limit of the City of London. There has been a building here since the thirteenth century. The gate that can be seen today was built by Sir Christopher Wren in the late seventeenth century.

Temple Bar was also a place of punishment, prisoners were kept here and pilloried and, more macabrely, the heads of traitors were displayed here on spikes as a warning to any would-be enemies of the sovereign. This barbaric practice was last employed in 1746.

Girl & Dolphin
ST KATHARINE'S WAY, E1

This sculpture by David Wynne was unveiled in 1972. The elegant lines of the bronze are a welcome sight, standing as it does in front of a rather ugly concrete hotel. Other sculptures by David Wynne can be seen throughout London. These include the bronzes *Boy With A Dolphin* on Cheyne Walk and *Girl With Doves* and *The Dancers* in Cadogan Place; and an early Wynne piece, *Guy the Gorilla* (suitably made from black marble), in Crystal Palace Park.

St Katharine's Way runs beneath Tower Bridge and along to St Katharine's Docks. Heading away from the docks, walkers find themselves at the cobbled area in front of the Tower of London, overlooking Traitors' Gate. Through this thirteenth-century river entrance, enemies of the State were taken by boat to be imprisoned in the Tower. Princess Elizabeth, later Queen Elizabeth I, was brought through Traitors' Gate in 1553. She was kept prisoner by her sister Mary, who attempted to convert her to Catholicism. Elizabeth spent two months imprisoned within the Tower Walls, though not solely confined to her cell; as a result, her favourite walking route in the gardens is still known as Princess Elizabeth's Walk.

The Horses of Helios
HAYMARKET, SW1

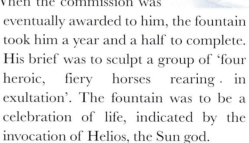

This magnificent fountain is entitled *The Horses of Helios*. The 4.2 metre-high horses were sculpted by Rudy Weller. They were originally modelled from clay, cast in fibreglass and moulded in sand before being finally cast in bronze; the basin is made of Baltic green granite. The fountain, part of the Criterion redevelopment, which was started in 1989, has become a 'wishing well' and each year a different charity is chosen to receive the profits.

Weller had already won one award for his sculpture, but he was up against the stiff competition of seven other leading sculptors for this prize. When the commission was eventually awarded to him, the fountain took him a year and a half to complete. His brief was to sculpt a group of 'four heroic, fiery horses rearing . in exultation'. The fountain was to be a celebration of life, indicated by the invocation of Helios, the Sun god.

Thomas Verity opened the Criterion Theatre in Piccadilly Circus in 1874, as a place for concerts and recitals. It was remodelled in 1902-03, but many felt that the bland, slapdash workmanship spoilt Verity's original design. When Criterion Developments Ltd were granted permission to redesign the site in the 1980s, they preserved the theatre's listed façade and remodelled the interiors and surrounding area.

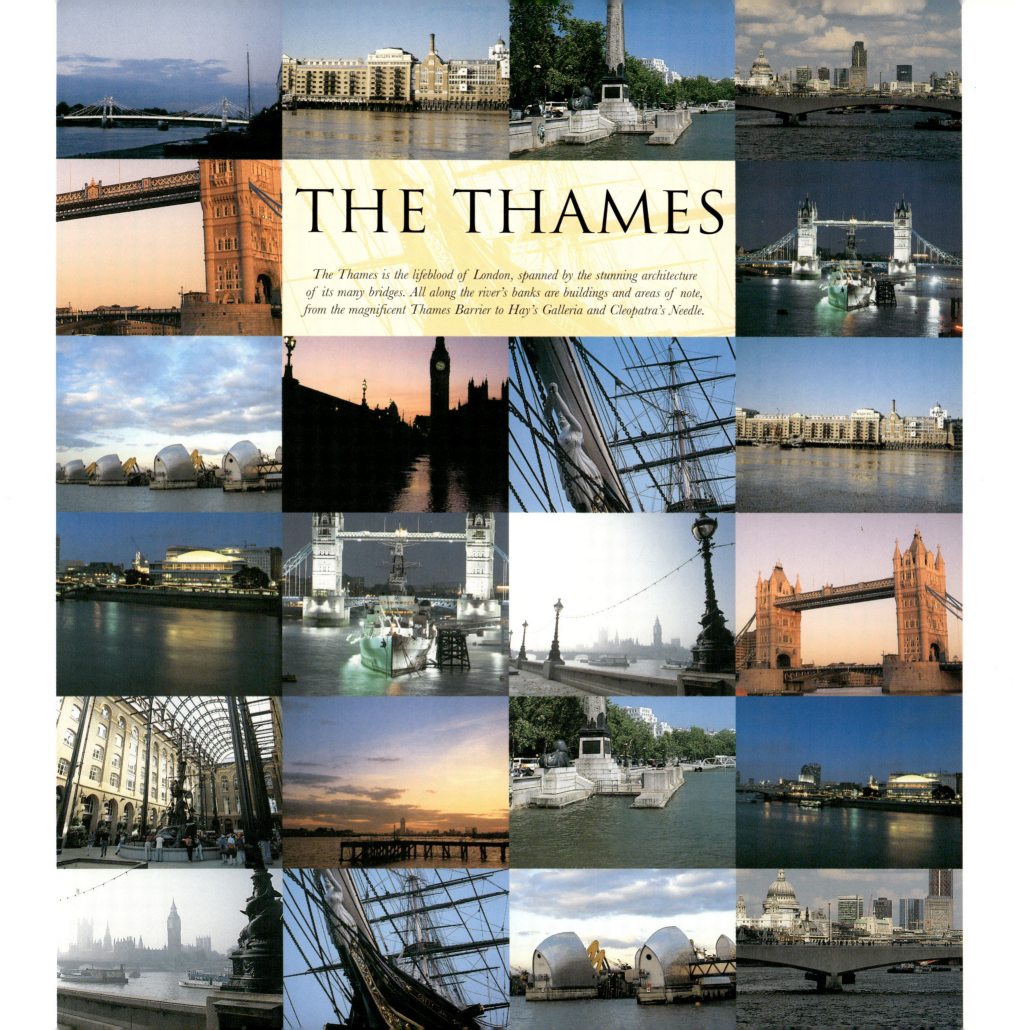

THE THAMES

The Thames is the lifeblood of London, spanned by the stunning architecture of its many bridges. All along the river's banks are buildings and areas of note, from the magnificent Thames Barrier to Hay's Galleria and Cleopatra's Needle.

Albert Bridge
CHELSEA, SW3

The sight of the Albert Bridge at night is one of the most beautiful that the Thames affords. The slender strings of lights that decorate the bridge's delicate-looking wrought-iron railings provide one of the most attractive night-time illuminations in the area.

The bridge was completed in 1873 to a design by R. M. Ordish. It was named after Prince Albert, by his still-mourning wife, Queen Victoria. Prince Albert died in 1861, but his loss affected Victoria until the end of her life in 1901. Many areas of London are named after him in an attempt to keep his spirit alive. The bridge that bears his name crosses the Thames at Chelsea and Battersea, near Battersea Park.

Not far from the Chelsea side of the bridge is the site of Henry VIII's old home, Chelsea Manor House. It was destroyed at the end of the eighteenth century, but some of the gardens have remained. It is said that many of the mulberry trees that still thrive in this area were planted by Henry's daughter, Elizabeth I.

Butler's Wharf
SE1

When London's docks were enjoying their heyday, Butler's Wharf was one of the most important; boats arrived from all over the world to unload their wares here. Merchant ships arrived from the East Indies and Latin America to supply England's foremost shops, restaurants and households with exciting new spices, exotic teas and aromatic coffees. Twenty-four hours a day workforces laboured to unload precious cargoes ready to be distributed all over the country and often to be shipped on abroad. Places such as Fortnum & Mason, the Savoy and St James's Palace were totally reliant on the industry of the dock workers in order to keep their own businesses and households going.

By the end of the nineteenth century, London's docklands began to fall into neglected disrepair. With the golden age of river transport at an end, the old wharves became sadly rundown. In the second half of the twentieth century, however, new developments began taking place and today Butler's Wharf is one of the Thames's liveliest spots once again. The old Victorian warehouses have been turned into luxurious new apartments and the ancient cobbled streets have become home to myriad shops, cafés, restaurants, museums and galleries.

Cleopatra's Needle
VICTORIA EMBANKMENT, WC2

The ancient Egyptians built obelisks as offerings to the Sun God, Ra; this one was constructed during the reign of Thuthmes III (*c.* 1500 BC) and erected during the festival of Sed. The inscriptions that can be seen on it, albeit slightly eroded after many years of lying beneath Egyptian sands, were added by Rameses the Great. Unlike Thuthmes, Rameses used the obelisk as a symbol of his own greatness, to record his many victories in war. During the reign of Cleopatra, the needle was taken to her city, Alexandria (*c.* 12 BC).

In 1819, Mahommed Ali, Viceroy of Egypt, presented the needle to Britain – the only problem being how to transport it here. The first ship to attempt to do so was the *Cleopatra*, in 1877; she ran into difficulties during a storm in the Bay of Biscay. Six of the crew were drowned and eventually the needle, encased in an iron covering, was abandoned at sea. In 1878, a crew commanded by John Dixon recovered the monument and brought it to England.

Before Cleopatra's Needle was finally placed here in 1878, a time capsule (including the day's newspaper and pictures of England's most beautiful women) was placed in the ground beneath the site where it would stand.

Lights Along the Thames
ALBERT EMBANKMENT, SE1

The strings of lights that decorate the Embankment, seen here in the late afternoon, are one of the most romantic sights in London when lit after dusk. Between them, Albert, Victoria and Chelsea embankments line both sides of the river and run for a total of three-and-a-half miles. The Albert Embankment, seen here, affords walkers a perfect glimpse of the Palace of Westminster, otherwise known as the Houses of Parliament.

The embankments were the work of the Victorian engineer, Sir Joseph Balgette. They took six years to complete and were finally opened to the public in 1874. At the same time, the Embankment Gardens were laid out – an idea first put forward by Sir Christopher Wren, 200 years previously, in 1666. All three provide pleasant walks, beautifully tended flower beds and sculptures in the heart of London's busiest areas and Victoria Embankment Gardens often play host to free open-air concerts and operas.

The Albert Embankment was built on the site of some of London's most ancient potteries, the Lambeth Potteries, which were in existence during the reign of Queen Elizabeth I.

HMS Belfast
SE1

HMS *Belfast* was the largest cruiser ever built for the Royal Navy; today she is moored permanently at Symon's Wharf between Tower Bridge and London Bridge. The proud ex-military cruiser was opened to the public in 1971 and now serves as a museum.

In times past, HMS *Belfast* was a vital part of the Royal Navy. She began her career in 1938 and saw much active service during the Second World War; she was particularly valuable at the Battle of North Cape and as part of the Normandy Landings. After the war, the cruiser remained an important naval addition until she was retired in 1965.

The ship measures 187 m (613 ft 6 in) from bow to stern, she weighs 11,553 tons and reaches a maximum speed of 32 knots (36 mph/58 kph) with ease. The shells from her guns weigh 112 lbs each and can travel to a range of 14 miles.

View from Charlton
SE18

This unusual view of London is taken from Charlton in the south-east of the city, near to the Thames Barrier. The skyline is dominated by Canada Tower, part of the Canary Wharf complex. The tower stands at a height of 250 m (800 ft), making it the tallest building in the British Isles.

Like many outer regions of London, the area of Charlton was once a small village and, under its early name of 'Cerletone', is mentioned in the *Domesday Book*. Apart from the enormous Thames Barrier, Charlton's main attraction is the splendid seventeenth-century Charlton House. It was built in 1612 and is one of London's best-preserved Jacobean homes. Its garden is home to an ancient mulberry tree that was planted by King James I in the early 1700s. The house is also believed to have been visited by the legendary architect Inigo Jones, who may well have contributed to Charlton House's design.

Tower Bridge
TOWER HILL, EC1

Before Tower Bridge existed, the only access to the other side of this part of the Thames was through a subway beneath the river; this was closed for public use shortly after the opening of the bridge in 1894. Today the bridge has a roadway for vehicles as well as pedestrian walkways. The sight from these is spectacular affording panoramic views over London.

The impressive Gothic edifice that has become one of London's best-known landmarks was designed by Horace Jones and built by the engineer John Wolfe-Barry. Building began in 1881 after the first stone had been laid by the Prince of Wales; it was he who declared the bridge open just three years later.

The bridge's clever construction allows the lower stretch of roadway to open up, thereby allowing tall ships access to this part of the Thames. When the bridge was first built, the roadway would open on average five times a day, moved by a powerful steam mechanism that remained in use until the 1970s. Today the bridge needs to be opened less often and the opening mechanism is electrified.

Thames Barrier
CHARLTON, SE18

The earliest recorded flooding of the Thames took place in the eleventh century and since then the river is known to have flooded its banks several times. The diarist Samuel Pepys records a flood that took place in 1663 and in just one decade of the nineteenth century, the river flooded three times. In the twentieth century London was flooded in 1928, when 14 people were drowned, and even more seriously in 1953, when over 300 people drowned. For a city with such a dense population another flood could have proved catastrophic. In the 1960s, the decision was made to construct a flood barrier.

The construction of the Thames Barrier was undertaken by the engineering firm Rendel, Palmer and Tritton, who began work on the project in the 1970s. The barrier was opened in October 1982 and the first time it protected the city against a potential flood was in February 1983.

From bank-to-bank, the Thames Barrier measures 520 m. It consists of 10 steel gates, including four main gates, and these are tested every month of the year – visitors are permitted to watch this magnificent sight.

South Bank Centre
SE1

The South Bank complex is a 27-acre site devoted to the arts. From this side of the river one can see St Paul's Cathedral to the east and the Houses of Parliament to the west. From the north side of the river, the South Bank can be reached by walking across either Waterloo or Hungerford bridges.

The many buildings which make up the South Bank Centre include the Royal Festival Hall, the Queen Elizabeth Hall, the National Theatre (made up of four separate theatres), the Hayward Gallery, the Museum of the Moving Image and the National Film Theatre. Throughout the year, South Bank is host to over 1,000 events, many of which are free.

In 1948, Clement Atlee's Labour government first broached the idea of holding a Festival of Britain. It was perceived as a 'tonic' to brighten the shell-shocked years after the Second World War. The Royal Festival Hall opened in 1951 to commemorate the 100th anniversary of the Great Exhibition. The first concert held there was attended by King George VI and Queen Elizabeth (now Queen Elizabeth, the Queen Mother).

View of the City
HUNGERFORD BRIDGE, WC2 & SE1

The view from Hungerford Bridge is one of the most impressive in London – one that even long-term residents never tire of. The instantly recognisable dome of St Paul's stands in the midst of London's most modern buildings; this impressive mixture of architecture highlights one the city's most endearing features, the ubiquitous mingling of the old and the new.

Hungerford Bridge links the Embankment on the north side of the river with the South Bank centre. The area that today makes up the South Bank became a centre of industry in the mid-eighteenth century. By 1775 the governing body of Lambeth had taken over what was formerly the site of a grand house, and built extensive waterworks here. In turn, these were taken over in the following century and the building became a brewery. During the Second World War, the brewery was badly damaged in the Blitz. The Royal Festival Hall now stands on its former site.

The Lion Brewery had, not surprisingly, two lions as mascots. One now stands a short distance away from its original site, at the southern entrance to Westminster Bridge. The second lion was chosen as a mascot for a different type of lion; today it welcomes rugby supporters to Twickenham's ground.

Night View of Westminster
WC1

The Palace of Westminster encompasses eight acres of land. It was created a royal residence in the time of William the Conqueror, when the Thames was a much bigger river and this part of London was an area of marshland outside the city. In medieval times, Westminster was known as 'Thorney' which means 'the island of briars'. The nearby Horseferry Road was, as its name suggests, a path to the horse-drawn ferry that took passengers to the Thames's islands at low tide.

The clock of Big Ben dominates this night-time view, with one of its four faces brilliantly lit up – each face requires 28 light-tubes to achieve full illumination. The tower that supports the clock, St Stephen's Tower, remarkably, was built from the inside outwards, requiring no form of scaffolding. The exterior is intricately carved in the Gothic style and the interior houses a secret – about a third of the way up is a small prison cell, intended for the use of disorderly parliamentarians. In 1902, the suffragette leader Emmeline Pankhurst was briefly imprisoned here.

On 9 December 1868, the world's first traffic lights were seen near here, on the corner of Whitehall and Bridge Street. The inventor was John Peake Knight.

Cutty Sark
GREENWICH, SE10

Whene'er to drink you are inclin'd,
Or cutty-sarks run in your mind,
Think, ye may buy the joys o'er dear,
Remember Tam o'Shanter's mare.

'Tam o'Shanter', *Robert Burns*

The *Cutty Sark* was once a fine merchant ship, used for transporting tea from China to London. She was named after Robert Burns's poem 'Tam O'Shanter'. The ship was made for the merchant Captain John Willis, and embarked on her first journey in 1869; she continued sailing the seas until 1938.

Tea was first introduced into England in *c.* 1656. It soon became popular in the smartest Society houses and, by the eighteenth century, the custom of afternoon tea had become an elaborate and formal ritual. In spite of its Eastern origins, tea became recognised as the staple drink of the English. Merchants, such as John Willis, became very wealthy due to the English obsession with tea.

Today the *Cutty Sark* is a fascinating museum documenting the lives of those who made their living working on the merchant ships. There is also a figurehead museum, where one can glimpse the supermodels of the eighteenth and nineteenth centuries sculpted and painted into ships' mascots.

Index